Lions on the Lawn

I sat the excited little lion, now about the size of a five-year-old child, in the centre of the sledge and hauled him along the rutted tracks to the hill known as Heaven's Gate. After an initial bout of nervous wavering, Marquis sat back and enjoyed the ride, purring his pleasure.

I sat up for the first few flashing hurtles down the hill, my feet steering the sledge and Marquis clutched safely in my lap, nervously licking my face.

The track was a fairly even and safe one, so we had no mishaps. We both enjoyed every moment of it, to the point that we must have made about thirty trips in all, shrieking and grunting our pleasure dementedly to each other in the otherwise deserted slopes, as we plunged breathlessly through diamond-flecked trees, all charcoal and red in the setting sun.

Also in Fontana

The Spotted Sphinx   *Joy Adamson*
Born Free   *Joy Adamson*
Living Free   *Joy Adamson*
The Animals Came in One by One   *Buster Lloyd-Jones*
Some of My Friends Have Tails   *Virginia McKenna*
Birds, Beasts and Relatives   *Gerald Durrell*
Beasts in My Bed   *Jacquie Durrell*

MARY CHIPPERFIELD

Lions on the Lawn

Collins
FONTANA BOOKS

First published by Hodder and Stoughton Ltd., 1971
First issued in Fontana Books 1972

© 1971 by Mary Chipperfield
All Rights Reserved

Printed in Great Britain
Collins Clear-Type Press
London and Glasgow

The articles on pp. 20-1 and pp. 72-3 are reproduced from
The Times by permission

The front cover photograph by John N. Pearson
is reproduced by kind permission of Bruce Coleman Ltd.

CONTENTS

ILLUSTRATIONS

Chapter One

MARQUIS, ORPHAN OF THE WILD

The little rejected lion was just a few hours old when he came into my life. Conceived in quarantine at Plymouth and subsequently free born, to parents from East Africa, he was the most precious waif I had ever rescued from an abandoned litter. He was in fact England's first stately wild cub and the premier Lion of Longleat, appropriately christened Marquis.

As I carried the helpless golden ball of spotted fur into the warm lounge of my home on that cold Sunday morning, 6 February, 1966, I had no idea whatsoever that this was to be the beginning of a unique animal-woman relationship.

All I knew at that moment was that this was a baby rejected at birth by his mother—a baby more dead than alive and requiring immediate succour if he was to survive at all. I handed the limp little velvet bundle to my husband, Roger, and ran to the kitchen. I quickly sterilized a feeding-bottle and prepared a quarter of an ounce of fortified milk, a feed sufficiently weak perhaps to keep him alive without straining his undernourished body.

The first few days of hand-rearing a lion cub are extremely critical times, especially if it has suckled on its mother. And Marquis had tasted the lioness's milk before she had thrust him away with her paw and stalked off to rejoin her pride. So, as I took him to me and inserted the teat of the bottle into his toothless wide mouth, I said a little prayer in my anxiety.

His eyes were open but they were deeply sunk, indicating that he was near the end of his strength; and they were still covered by a bluish film. His heart, beating against my own, seemed sound enough, but he weighed only two and a quarter pounds, which is just over half the weight of the average cub. It seemed improbable that Marquis could survive, but I was willing him to live. He just had to make it. Details of our Lions of Longleat reserve had just been announced to the press and the eyes of the world, some of them extremely critical, were turned upon this revolutionary Wiltshire wild-life sanctuary where our house, The Pheasantry, is situated.

My anxiety was doubled by the fact that Marquis's twin brother had died soon after birth. The birth of twins had in itself been somewhat unusual in that the average number of lion cubs in a litter is four, of which one usually dies soon after birth and another is often too weak to survive for long. Thus does Nature control the births of predators in the wild.

There was no response at first to the teat. Holding him in a nursing position, I joggled the bottle around in the soft pink mouth but he was apathetic. He seemed weary of life and ready to give up the ghost. I massaged his little belly, distended from hunger, in an attempt to get the digestive process working. But he scarcely stirred.

Desperate as the situation seemed, I decided I could make it no worse by attempting a risky short-cut. In the way a child is sometimes forced to swallow something nasty like castor oil, I took his too-warm nose in one hand and jerked it gently upwards so that his mouth opened wide. I then thrust the bottle in deeper, hoping his throat muscles would react positively and allow some of the milk to be swallowed.

It was a rough and dangerous thing to do. Marquis could have choked and that would have been the end of him. But mercifully the trick worked. Gulp, gulp, he went and suddenly he was sucking as well as gulping. In no time the bottle was empty. It seemed that once his stomach had accepted the milk it could not get enough of it. He went on sucking eagerly on the teat for minutes after the feed had gone. I did not dare give him more in case it was too much for him to keep down.

After what seemed an age, the deep sucking slowed and he gradually drifted into sleep. I rocked him in my chair for a time and when I was sure he had settled, I placed the poor little fellow in a well-padded cat basket my husband had dug out, a hot-water bottle by his side, and laid it in front of the log fire.

All through that seemingly endless Sunday Roger and I did nothing but sit and watch Marquis. Everyone else tiptoed about the house with long faces. The pets scarcely stirred.

Marquis's breathing seemed steady, but he sometimes stirred fitfully, as if in dreams. I had decided to feed him every two hours initially. On the second and third feeds, I again had difficulty in getting the sucking motion started. But by the late evening he was becoming more responsive and at midnight he woke naturally for the first time, apparently ready for his bottle.

We then ate for the first time that day ourselves, and I carried the basket, with its treasure, up to our well-heated bedroom and laid it across the foot of the bed where my feet would feel any vibration if he should be in distress.

Chapter Two

ANXIOUS DAYS

I scarcely closed my eyes all that long February night. I continued Marquis's weak feeds every two hours, and they went well. But my mind would not let me relax. At dawn I was standing by the wide bedroom windows, looking out across the green polar glow of the winter-shrouded wide acres of Longleat. Jigsaws of frost patterned the panes. The awakening scene was enlivened by the faint lazy sounds of estate workers stirring in a nearby cottage.

Birds were hopping around the garden, calling already for the bread and fats we invariably provided—robins, blackbirds, woodpeckers and jays; uncharacteristically fluttering in unison; brought together by the perishing cold. In the stables one of my horses neighed on waking and my mind registered the voice as that of High Endeavour.

Across the sparkling, motionless, wooded field beyond our home a fifteen-ton bulldozer stood crazily perched on the edge of a ditch, frozen mud jutting from its webbed feet, crouching menacingly, like a wounded dinosaur. A newly

erected fence had been transformed by frozen vapour into
a variegated confection of sugar. Half-completed roads were
patterned by frozen pools of water, over the largest of which
a pair of wagtails hovered, nonplussed by the silent hardness
of the crystal water.

It had been a severe and frustrating winter of wild winds
and heavy rains. Now frost had doubled the problems of the
small army of men who were struggling to complete, in time
for an Easter opening, the bones of the first African Game
Reserve to be created in an English country setting.

The game park, with the Lions of Longleat as its main
feature, had been the imaginative dream of my father, Jimmy
Chipperfield. The dream was now taking shape for him in
partnership with the Marquess of Bath. And my husband,
Roger Crawley, was to manage it.

Now that the drive-around park was so near completion, it
was vital that nothing should go wrong, and it was a matter
of pride as well as importance to all of us that Marquis, the
first Longleat lion, should be present in riproaring health for
Easter Monday weekend.

Indeed, Marquis was symbolic of the idea behind the project. Longleat was *not* a gimmick aimed at attracting more
visitors to one of the top ten stately homes, although it would
undoubtedly do that. It was a very serious endeavour to
allow people to study wild animals in something approaching
their natural state so that important lessons could be learned
about their conservation in a world more and more dedicated
to their destruction. Breeding would inevitably be a major
feature of such an adventure. And Marquis was an important
beginning, having been born to Longleat's first two imported
wild lions.

He was still asleep as the low weak sun first penetrated the
panes, so I slipped downstairs to see that the fire was alight
and to prepare his feed. The kitchen was already full of
steam billowing from a chattering kettle. Cook was up and
about before me. As I measured the feed, the milkman
arrived from the farm and already the creamy gallon in the
can was icing up. As he opened the door, the stabbing blast
of cold air that followed him in smelled like needles. 'Brrr!'

he said. 'It's polar bears you should be thinking of putting in the park, not bloody lions.'

It was scarcely the kindest thing he could have said to me at that moment. But he could not have known that a little son-loving African cub was upstairs fighting for life in the midst of one of the bitterest English days I could remember.

The fire in the sitting-room was blazing beautifully, so I called to Roger to bring Marquis down. The little chap looked much perkier this morning and gulped down his feed. The 'nappies' in the basket were wet for the umpteenth time since his arrival the morning before, but that was a good sign; his waterworks seemed in good order. As I removed the moist pad I noticed the soiling marks of his first stool and I put it on one side in case there were signs of tape worms or in case the vet might want to make an examination of it. Marquis's bowel movement had been soft, but not too runny, which was also a favourable sign.

Immediately after his feed, Marquis went back to sleep, so I was able to give my mind to the demands of the rest of my family of animals. In and around The Pheasantry I had assembled a private menagerie, for the breeding and training of animals had long been the prime purpose in my life. At that time it consisted of a dozen horses, a chimpanzee, a python, a sea-lion, an African elephant, an old donkey, a Shetland pony and seven dogs. In some ways, it was more an orphanage than a menagerie. Some of my animals had been taken in as 'strays', rejected, like Marquis, by their mothers, or had been wished on me by friends.

After a quick cup of coffee, I rushed out into the yard to see how my brood had fared in the bitter cold of the night. I need not have worried. My car, standing outside the house, looked like an iced cake, but Wamba the elephant was steaming gently in the warm garage and the horses in the stables had created their own central heating with the help of their straw bedding. Sean, the Great Dane; Henry, the Old English Sheepdog; Yula and Gipsy, the Alsatians; Winston and Brandy, the St Bernards, were all wagging their tails happily, excitedly voicing their usual good morning greetings and panting ghosts of frozen breath around them. Little

Amy, the cosseted Schnauzer, had ventured out of the house with me and was barking at the other six. I seemed to be the only suffering creature. I had wet eyes; I was blowing snorts of steam like a whale; and I was eating the wind with my teeth. My nose felt so dead that it hurt to breathe through it.

My brother, Richard, wrapped up like a Russian from the Siberian saltmines, clattered out of the house to begin a long day's work, directing the fencing and roadmaking in the reserve. 'East Africa, here I come,' he shouted cheerily and I chucked a horseshoe at him for fun and for luck.

The voluptuous sauna atmosphere of the horseboxes was welcome and my blood soon flowed warm again as I followed normal morning routine and carried armfuls of steaming muck out into the yard. Thereafter, as I worked, with brush and curry-comb, on the heaving, twitching, steaming flanks of the stallions, my mind was on Marquis and on the fifty other lions we would shortly be introducing to the wooded parklands across the fence.

Father had presented his scheme to Lord Bath at eleven a.m. on Saturday, 7 November, 1964, having decided that the ancient oak-strewn acres of Longleat were ideal for an animal sanctuary, and three weeks later a fifty-fifty partnership deal had been clinched. But it had taken more than a year to change a paper dream into an imminent reality. And, unwilling to trust the animal buying to anyone else, my father and I had, early in 1965, travelled thousands of miles through many countries in a few weeks choosing strong and healthy lions, likely to be adaptable to English conditions. Somehow, frost and snow had never entered my reckoning until now, and, although at that time the fifty incumbent Lions of Longleat were comfortably housed on a temporary basis at our zoos in Southampton and Plymouth, it might still be very cold in March when they were due to be moved to the park.

As I finished grooming the horses, Roger called out to me from the kitchen to say that Marquis was awake. I dropped everything. Someone else could take the hay and bread to the elephant for once and the dogs would just have to forego their morning run around the estate. And Charles, the chimp, could jump up and down as much as he liked. There would be no 'walkies' for him either that day.

It took but a moment to prepare a slightly stronger feed of Ostermilk. Marquis's stomach had seemed settled enough at six a.m. for me to risk increasing the dose. I had laid in cod liver oil and other fortifiers, but it was much too soon to add these to his bottle.

I took him in my lap and was thrilled to find the bony body to be much livelier. His mouth was opening and closing like a hot wet orchid and he immediately responded to the teat, with a gurgling in his throat and a soft look of pleasure on his face. Young wild cubs, contrary to general belief, can change their facial expressions from fear to boredom to pleasure, according to their moods, but I was nevertheless surprised and delighted to see so young and precious a baby with a look of gratified contentment on his fox-like features. So hard did he go at his milk that some of it dribbled down on his little goatee beard.

The vet called after breakfast. I had rung him the day before but he had been involved in a difficult birth fifty miles away and had been unable to attend on Marquis sooner. Not that this greatly mattered. I had been brought up with lion and other cubs since childhood, whereas this was his first encounter with one. He took Marquis's temperature and pulse, looked at his tongue and eyes, and examined his thin body and the sparse hair of his shaggy coat. 'He seems to be pulling through,' was all he would say, 'but it will be a few days before you can be sure that he'll make it. I'd say he has no more than a forty-sixty chance.' My intuition had led me to much the same conclusion. I have natural 'bush eyes' and ears, and can receive information from an animal by vibrations I cannot explain.

I showed the vet the fouled bedding. As we looked at it together, it was apparent that there were tiny worms in it. 'We can't do anything about these in his present condition,' said the vet simply. 'He'll have to build his strength before he can keep down powders as well as feeds.' Before he left, the vet nicked Marquis's ear and took a small blood sample on a slide for examination.

The rest of the day passed slowly, anxiety dominating the mood, and for a second night I slept little. There was little improvement, but Marquis was certainly no worse. It was as much as we could hope for at this stage.

Chapter Three

LIONS, LIONS EVERYWHERE

Somehow, we got through the first week with the 'sick baby', our nerves ragged from lack of sleep. By the seventh day, another Sunday, Marquis had gained two ounces and appeared to be out of danger. His pulse and temperature were normal and the blood sample had shown him to be free from disease. This was just as well, for other lions would now be arriving almost daily for their settling-in period in the reserve, and our hands were needed for many specialized tasks.

At first, Marquis had tended, in his waking moments, to hide his face from everything that went on but now, although still more in his basket than out of it, he was beginning to take an interest in his surroundings, and particularly in the animals that came and went from the house.

Yula, my four-year-old Alsatian bitch, had been unusually attracted to Marquis from the start and in the past two days had begun to show a positively motherly affection and guardianship for him. After his feed, and while he was still in my lap, she would lick him all over with her long tongue, which he seemed to like and which appeared to energise him a little. Perhaps her saliva had some healing reviving qualities of which we sophisticated humans know nothing.

Indeed, after one such demonstration of affection, he licked her back with his rough little tongue and then began weakly licking his own paws for the first time. This was progress indeed.

Out in the park, Lord Bath, Father and Richard were digging, hauling trees and inserting hardcore in the miles of roads around which visitors were to drive in only a few weeks' time. The entrance toll-gates to the reserve were being constructed a stone's throw from The Pheasantry. Work was running late, because of the bad weather, and we were all rather anxious. But if long hours and dedicated work counted for anything, the last detail would be completed by the week before Easter.

Already, we were being surprised daily by casual visitors, which did not make things any easier. Cars would arrive snoopily at the entrance to our home; picnickers would squat on the high ground watching the men at work and probably hoping to see the first lion. People being what they are, some of these sightseers were no doubt hoping to see fights between animals, or even a human being attacked.

Lions of Longleat was an awesome project in a way. We were really out on a limb proposing to let wild animals loose in Wiltshire. We had tremendous faith in what we were attempting. But our detractors had outnumbered our supporters from the start. In particular, the 'old Thunderer', *The Times*, had sharply rapped our knuckles and had set up howls of protest in Parliament and in other important bastions of the establishment.

There had been suspicions that we had pulled a confidence trick by getting planning permission for the project in an underhand way. In fact, what had happened was that cautiously worded letters had been sent from Longleat to the appropriate county offices at an early stage requesting permission to erect 'a fence to restrict the movement' of certain unspecified animals. Whether the council actually knew what was in the wind is debatable. But the application was approved without reservation.

A guarded statement to the press had been the next move. This was to the effect that the fenced-off area would enclose England's first lion park. This was received with incredulity, nationally and locally. Cartoonists had a field day. 'Little Albert' records were re-issued. Leader writers filled their pens with vitriol. One local councillor back-pedalled hastily by saying, 'Good God! I thought the fence was for deer!'

But it was the Old Lady of Printing House Square who set the goat among the lions in a leading article which ran as follows:

Sporting competition between owners to make their stately homes and broad-acred parks the mostest for visitors is all very well. But there are limits, and in proposing to enlarge a pride of lions in a compound on his Wiltshire estate, the Marquess of Bath has overstepped them. No amount of soothing assurances that the fences would be too high to be jumped, the visitors warned to stay put in their cars, and that the game wardens roaming day and night would be crack shots, can persuade sensible people that a quite gratuitous and unnecessary risk to life is not contemplated. Up till now the man-eating propensities of lions in England have happily been left in the realm of light verse, of Mr Stanley Holloway's little lad Albert who was swallowed whole and the Bellocian little gentleman whom Ponto got. But there was the grim case in 1956 of the ten year old Boy Scout who died after being mauled by a lion at Whipsnade. How long will it be, if Lord Bath has his way, before that tragedy is re-enacted?

The fecklessness of a minority of the great British public knows no bounds, and who will deny that sooner or later a fatal accident is likely to occur? A start is planned with fifty of the great beasts. But allowances have been made for this number to be doubled by breeding. This is one of the most fantastically unsuitable uses for a stretch of England's green and pleasant land that can ever have entered the head of a noble proprietor. The wildest follies of the past pale before it; the old landlords, though they had some odd ideas, seldom lost their feel for their native soil. They seldom went in for stunts.

Lions in an African game reserve are at home. A few at Whipsnade and at Regent's Park, under the auspices of the Zoological Society, are justified. But a lion in Wiltshire is as out of place as a Wodehousian Empress of Blandings pig would be in Kruger Park. Cattle, sheep and deer ought to be good enough for a Wiltshire man. The proper place for lions in an island that is spared them in the wild state is heraldry. Although some planning permission has inexplicably been given, there is still time for wiser counsels to prevail. Lord Bath's dangerous folly is not due to be open to the public until next Easter. Ordinary citizens who seek to make modest changes on their property are often checked by a miscellany of planners with power. Here if ever is a just cause for official intervention—if necessary from Whitehall.

The Times, 2 September, 1965.

To his eternal credit, Lord Bath never lost his nerve, as lesser men might have done in the face of this denunciation and, as for the rest of us, there's nothing like opposition for making Chipperfields stick gamely to their plans.

The lions chosen for Longleat had been bought in Europe, the Middle East and Africa. Even with our excellent and longstanding connections with circuses, zoos and dealers, it had been no easy task to round up fifty good specimens. We must have looked at and handled hundreds of lions. There was no shortage of them in numbers, but the quality had been less impressive. Many we had rejected at once because they were mangy, had abnormalities of build or were obviously dangerous.

The cost of the animals was something around £10,000, which was within our budget. Apart from the fact that everything had to be ready for the following Easter at Longleat, our mission had had to be carried out quickly and secretly because, once the news of our buying quest had got around the animal dealers, it would have been much more difficult to strike keen bargains. There were several sorts of lions involved. There were the smaller Plains ones, native to Rhodesia, and the larger ones from the forests of Abyssinia, as well as the more common Gold Coast lions.

Eventually, time ran out on us, overshadowed by quarantine schedules, before we had quite made our quota and we had to buy a group of five lions 'blind' by correspondence from the Jerusalem Biblical Zoo. As it happened, these turned out to be some of the finest we had ever handled, so we were lucky.

While Father and I had been away, my brother, Richard, had been busy at our Southampton zoo, having every available cage checked and passed for quarantine by the Ministry of Agriculture. Even so, by the time crates began arriving from many points east and north, it had become a problem to find places for the incomers and never in history can a small zoological garden have housed such a largesse of lions.

Quarantine (which was then six months, but is now a year) does not prohibit public access, at a suitable distance; so that late summer of 1965, the many seasonal visitors to our zoo were often heard to say, as they passed from cage to cage, 'Not *another* bloody lion . . .' The same situation prevailed at our zoo at Plymouth (which was already registered as a quarantine station) but on a lesser scale.

Alas, cat enteritis had claimed two imported cubs, despite my very best nursing efforts, and one of the lionesses, bought unseen, died of old age.

There was still time to rush in a few more, so Richard went off to Africa (having heard that the filming of *Born Free* had just ended) and chose seven excellent animals that had appeared in the epic. Although I hate to say it (priding myself, as I do, on my own shrewdness) this was the best buy ever made in the family. Richard got them for £10 each, plus the cost of air-freighting them to England. The average price of a lion is about £200. No wonder the film industry is ailing!

Father, with plenty of other problems to occupy him, put me in charge of all the lions destined for Longleat. Working with them, while they were in quarantine, I got to know each one individually—their characters, personalities and quirks. To this day, I can recognize each one instantly and they know me when I call them.

Over-confidence, in those crowded days at Southampton and Plymouth, led to one of my more serious injuries. Since babyhood I have had my share of bites and scratches and have accepted them as part of the job. They have usually been my own fault, as was the case on this occasion. Wotan was one of my favourites among the fifty imported lions. I could do anything with him. But one day I broke my rule of watchfulness and he underlined a fact I have always known —that you can never truly trust a full-grown wild animal, and especially a male one.

As was my wont, one day I was stroking his nose through the bars of the quarantine cage. Just at that moment, a member of the public came up behind me and spoke. I started at the sound and turned my head. Instantly, Wotan, who had also been frightened by the sudden arrival of the stranger, snapped nervously, and succeeded in biting off the tip of the third finger on my right hand. What really annoyed me was that he also ate it!

Fortunately, he did not have rabies and the wound healed successfully. There was so much to do that I was back at work within an hour or so.

One by one and two by two, as their quarantine periods ran out, I now began transporting the lions from Southampton and Plymouth to Longleat. Unlike Marquis, who had been the first to make the journey, I delivered them direct to the enclosure, where we installed them in temporary 'cages' to begin their acclimatization. These had to be roomy and comfortable, because the size of an animal relative to its environment and the adequacy of its living-quarters affect its moods. Lions confined in too small a space can become destructive or wicked out of sheer frustration.

We were attempting something no one had ever tried in England before, so the initial confinement in large, safe huts was a necessary precaution that allowed for careful, studied preparation.

The sound of other lions roaring a few hundred yards away had an interesting effect on Marquis, who was now entering his second week at The Pheasantry. He found his own voice and delighted us with his little, squeaky attempts to answer his kin. From then on, we knew he was gaining in strength of spirit as well as body by the increasing vehemence of his infantile growls and snarls. He even spat occasionally at strangers. This was a great relief and joy.

Wild lions roaring to each other at night is an awesome

sound, but it had a special significance at Longleat and re-
presented for us another step nearer the ideal of the open
lion park.

It has always seemed to me, by the way, that there is a considerable field of research open to someone prepared and
able to analyse and translate the vocal sounds of the wild.
Each animal speaks with as individual a voice as does each
and every human. Some of their communications I understand. I would like to know more.

The vet came in most days, as fascinated as I was with
Marquis's reactions to diet and care. I had lengthened the
feeding intervals to three hours and his bottle now contained
baby-milk, laced with vitamins, glucose, calcium and a little
egg-yolk.

'You know,' the vet told me on the tenth day of my nursing, 'it's more than the food and attention that's bringing him
round. It's the love. A baby animal, even more than a human
baby, can sense whether you really love it. I suppose it can
scent it, just as it can scent fear. You have made Marquis
feel secure and wanted. That's what we all need when we're
little, whatever species we belong to.'

'Have another toasted scone,' I teased, and went off to
exercise my horses.

Chapter Four

MARQUIS AND THE ALARM CLOCK

No sooner were Longleat's fifty lions safely installed in their
huts for the settling-in period than the frost, which had been
absent for a week, returned fit to freeze the marrow in the
animals' bones. We were thankful at least that it would be a
week or two yet before they would have to be released into
the park. The huts were well-insulated and liberally carpeted
with warm straw and the inmates seemed content to eat,

sleep and ruminate.

Outside, in the shimmering crystal kingdom of the reserve, all was not yet ready for the royal prides. From many points across the ragged wildness of frost-bitten turves came the sounds of buzz saws and of hammering. Stakes were being driven into unyielding iron-hard mud; brambles were being rooted out; and 'plains' were being cleared.

Wielding their sharp seven-pound axes, bill-hooks, cross-cut saws and wedges, foresters were lopping branches and removing occasional trees so that the winding road through the reserve would afford motorists unrestricted views of the action. This particular activity was being supervised as usual by Henry Frederick Thynne, the sixth Marquess of Bath. Trees are one of his passions and he is an extremely able forester. To see him plant a tree is a joy. He handles young seedlings as tenderly as if they are newly hatched birds and places them gently but firmly into nests his fingers have made in the soil. All over the estate are perspectives of bristling skylines, arches and shaded glades of trees he planted in his youth and since as a continuing contribution to the beautiful symmetry of the well-wooded estate lovingly created and nurtured by generations of Thynnes. The necessary removal of some of his beloved trees as a preliminary to the wild life venture must have been causing him some pain, as we feel pain at the loss of any of our animals. But he was seeing to it that disturbance to the wooded areas was kept to a minimum.

Longleat, 'the treasure-house of the west', came into being in 1580, when the magnificent Italian Renaissance-style Elizabethan house was built by black-bearded Sir John Thynne, and it has been lived in ever since by members of the family. The Thynnes, to a man, have devoted themselves over the centuries to improving and beautifying their home and estate, and an important landmark as far as the latter is concerned was the decision of the first marquess to employ Capability Brown to redesign the site (once a monastery) and its surrounding park. The landscaping is undoubtedly one of Brown's greatest triumphs and affords a fabulous setting for the game reserve.

The Pheasantry, too, has an attractive history and, appropriately, 100 years or so ago its high walls enclosed a collection of kangaroos kept by the Marquess of the time for study and breeding. Before we arrived, in 1966, The Pheasantry had long served the function covered by its name and had also been for a time the residence of Lord Bath's sister. Pheasants are still raised on the estate but are bred at a suitable distance from the lions, who can be partial to baby game birds.

The Pheasantry is a cosy and yet a spacious gracious house, with few cold corners, so my pets and strays were little concerned with the icy February world outside. With Marquis losing his three-paws-in-the-grave look but scarcely out of danger, my nights and days were still continuing periods of nursing care punctuated by three-hourly feeds plus re-filling of the hot-water bottle, and the careful cosseting of the frail little fluffy golden Teddy-bearish baby generally. The sacks of sweet-scented wood chips and logs Richard brought in from the forestry operation, together with candy-brittle beech twigs, provided constant aromatic fires which all domesticated animals and most humans relish.

Marquis would get out of his basket occasionally after the first week and totter around clumsily, but he could not walk far without losing his balance. His eyes had not yet learned to focus properly and he would stumble into furniture. On all such occasions, Yula, the Alsatian, would stand by, anxiously and protectively whining warnings to the little cub. This was just another revelation to us of the many remarkable facets of Yula's character. I bought her from a Plymouth policeman when she was three and a half. She was fully trained as a police dog, but had been rejected by the force because she was a bit nervous of one particular drill—getting a man out of a dark building. She is the perfect watchdog. If the office in The Pheasantry is unmanned at any time, she is ferocious and will not allow anyone in except a member of the family. Yet she is sweetness itself with children, other pets and visitors, as long as we are around to let her know that things are normal. She is also a talented film and television performer, faultless in all she is asked to do.

When Marquis grew tired from the exertions of staggering

a few yards across the carpet, he would climb on top of the ever-willing Yula and the two would curl up in dreams together, as snug in their togetherness as twin-podded chestnuts.

Marquis was now on full-strength Ostermilk, with egg, glucose, vitamins and calcium added. Mostly he had his feed in my lap. He would close his eyes and roll his head from side to side with pleasure when gulping the milk and would squeeze the bottle rhythmically with his front paws, as though kneading his mother's belly to hasten the flow. Often Yula would lick his face to clean the milk away. Lazy by nature, like all lions, he would suck my fingers for a few minutes after the feed and would soon be asleep.

Lions have sharp claws from the day they are born, so these have to be cut back with nail snippers regularly or there would not be much left of my clothes during feeding sessions. Like all cats, lion cubs are wonderfully clean, sweet-smelling creatures, but they usually want to widdle or clear their bowels as soon as they wake. I began training Marquis, after the first anxious days, by taking him to a newspaper as soon as he stirred. He soon accepted this as the natural way to do things. Inevitably, there were occasional accidents but he disliked them as much as I did, so I did not have to rub his nose in them. When there was an accident the disgust he expressed made me dissolve into laughter.

We take the 'quality' newspapers daily, and on Sundays, for very good reasons. Indeed, I have always meant to write glowing, unsolicited testimonials to the editors of *The Times*, the *Daily Telegraph*, the *Sunday Times* and the *Observer*, saying that they have no equals . . . for absorption. The 'popular' papers are less effective soaker-uppers and the glossy magazines are of no use at all.

This use of newspapers, in animal toilet-training, causes occasional quarrels in the family. We are avid collectors of newspaper cuttings and pictures of animals, with the result that there is general fury if one of us puts a paper into use on the floor before snipping has taken place.

Eating and sleeping were the main features of Marquis's young life, but, in the second week, he began to take a welcome interest in toys. His favourite was a little rabbit, with a weight in the base, which when knocked over always sprang back to its squatting position. The other animals accepted that this was Marquis's toy and it was always handy by his basket for when he felt strong enough to play.

Just like human babies, cubs like something to cuddle. Usually a hot-water bottle suffices in the early stages, but before he was two weeks old, Marquis made his own choice. Someone brought in a brightly coloured alarm clock one day for the cook to use and it lay on the floor for a bit, where Marquis discovered it during one of his perambulations. Its tick fascinated him and he had soon lain down on top of it and gone to sleep. From then on, the alarm clock, always ticking its comfort, was his constant cuddly companion, in his basket and in our bed. And a new one had to be purchased for cook.

Every night, Marquis would curl up in our bed and every three hours I would be up and about, preparing his feed and assuring myself that he was all right.

'It's worse than having a real baby,' my husband would grumble sleepily.

'We are,' I told him one night. I was six weeks pregnant.

Chapter Five

TIGER IN THE LION'S HOME

A new arrival at The Pheasantry when Marquis was two weeks old diverted a certain amount of attention from him. I had been in the habit of buying from London Zoo any animals they had hand-reared and could spare. They now offered me a tiger cub and I accepted at once. Kumar was ten weeks old, off the bottle and house-trained. He was eating meat with tremendous appetite and weighed something around 20 lbs.—about five times as much as Marquis.

Kumar never fouled his box from the day he arrived and

was soon trotting out into the garden dutifully for all evacuations. His teeth were the biggest worry. Unlike claws, these cannot be blunted and in the first few days, until we could cuff him into understanding right and wrong, his razor-sharp 'pearlies' wrought havoc with furniture and furnishings. In his exploration of the house, he had many falls from high objects, that must have seemed like precipices to his young eyes, but his bones seemed to be made of indiarubber and he would bounce away to find out more and more about his strange new world. All wild animals examine their 'territory' in this way immediately on arrival.

In the wild, Kumar would have been groomed several times a day by his mother's rough tongue. In The Pheasantry, this was just another task I had to take on—washing his paws, wiping his eyes and brushing his soft, stripy fur until it shone. It emerged, fortunately, that Kumar was good-natured, and he put up with all this and the occasional bath with a tolerant amiability.

Tigers are much more valuable creatures, in monetary terms, than lions, and can cost five or six times as much for a good specimen. They are supposed to be more difficult to raise in Europe, but I have never found this to be so. Granted, the smaller Malay tigers (to which family Kumar belongs) are accustomed to a humid climate and do not take to our cold winters as easily as the big Bengal ones. But tigers are always fascinating to have around—true aristocrats and perhaps the most intelligent of the cat family.

They are not, as is often said of them, treacherous. But they can be highly strung and nervous in their bravery. They are also less predictable and more cunning than other cats; less easy to 'read' Lions have perhaps the greatest wealth of expression among mammals, which top the lists for articulation. Lions, from babyhood, can produce almost exaggerated expressions and cries. You can look at them, as you would look at a young child with a limited vocabulary, and know what they are trying to say. Indeed, with some superior lions, like Marquis, you get to feel that they regard humans as rather slow on the uptake; so much so that they constantly try to offer elementary lessons in the meaning of animal expressions. Tigers (like lions' other close relatives, leopards and pumas) can be expressive, too, but are more secretive and take longer to 'read' They need discipline and have to be watched more carefully than lions, as the pets in the house recognized instantly with Kumar. He even formed the habit of walking backwards from them in his early days because of some inbuilt suspicions about their behaviour.

Cats generally cannot be bluffed. They can sum up other animals and humans instantly and are able to sense fear or trust instantly. Tigers can be fiercely affectionate and the first signs that they are willing to be friendly come in a curious form of blowing—a noise, rather like the snorting of a horse, which they make with their lips. Another fascinating difference from lions, which fits in with their characters, is that tigers are *always* born with their eyes open, whereas lion cubs vary in this respect.

Kumar soon got to know and respect us. I stroked him gently whenever he approached me—on the top of his head, along his muzzle and behind his ears. All cats like that. And all the while I talked to him soothingly, making him feel welcome and wanted. The first time he met Marquis, they both spat a bit, but after individual scoldings, they began to accept each other. Lions are suspicious of anything new, so Marquis had to come in for even more talking to than the tiger.

In the third week, Marquis's nose was threatened with being put even more out of joint with the arrival at the huts in the park of several more litters of Longleat lions. I had had to be particularly watchful during their pregnancies in case the lionesses had been upset by the move and by the cold weather. In the event, three babies were rejected by their mothers out of three litters totalling twelve cubs, which was a normal average, and I brought all the orphans home to The Pheasantry, much to Marquis's disgust.

We named them Major, Lisa and Sheba. The male cub's eyes were open and we noticed immediately that he had a squint—very unusual among cats. Roger took an instant liking to the little fellow and more or less took him over from birth, which certainly did not displease me, from the work point of view. All three had been rescued from the straw before they had sucked their mother's milk, so they took to their bottles and thrived more quickly than Marquis. Indeed, within a few days they were crawling around waywardly, and it sometimes seemed impossible to walk anywhere in the house without tripping over or treading on one of the squirming furry bundles.

The weather had suddenly improved so, early in March, Kumar was banished to the garden, first on a long chain and then on a running wire. He had so much energy that he wore the blades of young grass down as soon as they came through and eventually churned the would-be lawn into mud. But he had to remain there because a fourth 'orphan' arrived from the huts on 10 March. This was another attractive but unloved cub which we called Simba, which is African for lion. My maternal instincts were certainly being fuelled well in advance of the arrival of my own baby. A motherless lamb also joined the family at The Pheasantry about this time and confirmed the biblical prophecy by being brought up among lions.

Chapter Six

THE FREEDOM OF LONGLEAT

By this time spring had succeeded in rolling up winter's spiky carpet. Mild rain and clear clean sunlight had begun to transform the sadly shrivelled scene. New life could be heard under high hedgerows. Early crocuses were attracting pecking birds to their beds at the lawn's edges, despite Kumar's daunting presence. Elsewhere in the garden, green spears heralding golden daffodils were already a good foot high. Everywhere buds were ready to burst joyously from briar and hawthorn. Soon there would be blossom in the orchard.

Out in the exposed parts of the lion park only dandelions had appeared so far, but up in the mossy banks of the wood, fern fronds were straightening up to protect expected brigades of bluebells and companies of primroses.

It seemed silly, at such a delightfully pregnant moment in the gentle cycle of the English seasons, to be thinking of rampant lions rampaging across this pastoral landscape. But the freeing of the lions was now so near at hand that it was excluding all else from our minds.

In the reserve, the last stake was in place; the final 'dummy run' had been made with the lions' meat waggon; and the drive-around road for the customers, winding like a maniac-doodler's squiggle, from The Pheasantry to nigh-on Longleat House and back, was firm and well-drained.

A Monday in mid-March, less than three weeks before Easter, had been chosen as 'release day'. I awoke to a perfectly clear sky and the promising sign of rooks flying high. I slipped out of the sheets quietly, as I had done several times during the night. Marquis had taken to sleeping deeply between feeds and Roger had always been a bit of a Rip Van Winkle. Curled up together, they seemed to be nuzzling each other's warmth in the safety of the big bed, snug as mice in a hayrick. Marquis was now breathing easily and making soft drinking sounds in the pillow. My quick look brought me a sharp thrill of pleasure that the little lion was so obviously well.

Downstairs in the fire-flushed warmth of the sitting-room I laid out fresh newspapers for the other cubs, fed them and left them curled up in their baskets like salted snails. Then I dashed through the kitchen, shouting orders to cook for the family lunch that was to precede the adventure in the reserve. A rich pink ham was already steaming on a dish by the window and great slabs of fresh butter, patted and enscrolled, had arrived from the farm. Gulping a pot of steaming coffee on my way, I headed out across the yard towards the stables, past my barking dogs and the chattering chimp, greeted also en route by Donja the elephant, trumpeting like a wounded fire-engine, causing the hens to rise like windy paper-bags as they shed feathers in all directions.

The spring air was like a draught of cool lager. Tits were 'see-see-seeing' in the highest trees, eyes sharp for the first sight of tit-bits. A badger ambled across the approach road, idly kicking up his heels as he sniffed the air for his breakfast. Among tufts of new grass at the side of the yard near the black alp of horse manure a small bird's body lay where it had fallen at the height of the frost; now it was more like a cage of old sticks than the warm living creature it had been so recently.

As I reached the stables, a young girl groom arrived, alive with pink cheeks, dark eyes and hair as unbridled as the mane of an unbacked colt. My voice was still half-edged with sleep, I told her which horses to tackle first and I got on with the mucking out. Everything had to be ready by the time my father arrived from Southampton, so that full attention could be given to his instructions for the freeing of the lions.

God, it was a lovely morning for the great occasion. As I carried in the horses' hay in armfuls of sweet-smelling embalmed summer fragrances, it dawned on me that I should be feeding Marquis again, but just then Roger arrived downstairs, tousled, tall and boyish, to reassure me that all was well and that he was taking care of the other breakfasts—Marquis, Kumar, the lamb, the sea-lion, the chimp, the snake and the dogs. I got on with the grooming as though my life depended on it and had changed into fresh clothes, practical but feminine, by the time my father's Rolls-Royce rattled across the cattle-grid at the gate.

The conference that followed was brief and to the point. We had converted the large french-windowed morning-room of The Pheasantry into an office and as lions played games with dogs on the newly-carpeted floor, Father, immaculate as ever, ran through the drill. He is an astonishing man, efficient and practical as he is imaginative . . . a leader born. Nobody dreams when Jimmy Chipperfield talks.

He had drawn up a neat map, covering the area of the action. We were all given our battle-stations and duties. Guns were checked and issued. It was all very matter-of-fact, with no hint that the drill related to a venture as new as a flight into space.

Lunch passed quietly and quickly. We were all imagining the moment when the puzzled lions would emerge from their scattered huts to nose around the vast acres of the reserve, scarcely believing the extent of their freedom. It was an awesome thought; so much planning and nurturing towards this moment of truth. We were about to move into the unknown; from the safe earth-orbit to the unknown moon-path.

Release hour was to be two thirty p.m. Just after two, Richard brought a zebra-painted safari Land-Rover round to The Pheasantry entrance and we all climbed aboard, rifles clutched at safe angles.

Everywhere in this shrinking world, wild creatures are daily being shot, trapped or squeezed out of their natural territories by mankind on the march. We were about to institute a small but not insignificant reversal of this sickening trend. We were proposing to give something back to nature, to launch an East African Game Reserve in one of the few areas of the English countryside that had escaped destruction by industrial sprawl and spread. If the lions accepted life among the dandelions of the Longleat meadow, many other wild species were to be added. But would their leonine behaviour be as calm in balmy Wiltshire as we had hoped and prayed? We would soon know.

In no time we had taken up our positions and Father was fingering his watch. A light breeze had sprung up. The lions roared from their three main huts, sensing something afoot, and the trees whispered back from the hill, murmuring in gentle seas of sound. It was the perfect setting for a royal hunt in the sun, but the last thing we wanted was to have to use our guns which were only for our ultimate protection if all else failed.

Marquis should have been with me, I felt, but he was still too young and too frail to be exposed to so dramatic an occasion. The official opening in the week before Easter would be a different matter and I hoped to see to it that Longleat's very first lion would be present and correct then.

Father did not appear to be nervous, so I tried hard not to fret as the seconds ticked away. I wondered what thoughts were going through his alert mind at this crucial moment in what was likely to be his greatest achievement to date. Was he brooding over the fact that most of the family fortune, built up over many hard years of animal dealing, training and showing, was encompassed in this bold throw? Was he recalling that his father-in-law, my maternal grandfather, had been killed by a lion in a moment of unwatchfulness? Was he still measuring the chances of success and failure and with them the inevitable reactions of the many prophets of doom now waiting in the wings hoping for disaster? Outwardly he was showing no emotion whatsoever, but I could well imagine his inner anxieties. Father was rather in the position of Noah as he led his animals to the Ark while all about him thought him a fool.

He now gave a signal on the compact radio transmitter-receiver he was carrying and an armed patrol vehicle began to move around the double perimeter fence, ready to deal with any emergency there, from outside or inside. Uninvited visitors were squatting on the ground and even in trees overlooking the reserve, like vultures gathering for the kill.

· We were intent on recreating opportunities, absent for centuries from England, for the study of wild animal behaviour in fairly natural conditions. But before that worthy plan could proceed we had to test the lions' behaviour ourselves. Roger, Richard, the chief game warden, Mike Lockyer, and a few of the more highly trained wardens we had recruited had their hands on the bolts of the cages, ready for Father's ultimate signal.

My mind flipped ahead. These were my lions, chosen by me and cared for by me. I felt a bit like royalty on this right royal occasion. I saw myself indulgently and patronizingly patting the beasts' heads as they came out, like a queen in an orphanage.

At that moment, Father raised his rifle, we all became as watchful as snipers, the hut doors opened and the lions were free. That moment had a sharp salt taste I still remember. But the action was very different from how I had pictured it. In the manner of greyhounds in a race, the three groups, totalling fifty lions, bounded out of their cages, neither looking to left nor to right. Instantly cashing in on weeks of bottled-up energy, they galloped straight off in all directions, clawing at turves and clumps of dandelion as they went.

It was then that a fascinating early glimpse of future behaviour among the Lions of Longleat was given to those of us privileged to watch this first flight to freedom. Without pause, each and every lion headed single-mindedly for the perimeter of the reserve, as if answering a signal only they could hear. When they got to the fence, those of my lions which had been brought up in zoos started to pace up and down a short length of it, sniffing the air in case of danger. They had 'adopted' a cage area which suited them and were defending it, instinctively resuming their normal captive habits.

But the younger lions, less set in their ways, immediately tried to escape.

As we watched, frozen by surprise, a number of them succeeded in scrambling under the strands of barbed wire which made up the inner fence, tearing their amber coats but disregarding the pain in their struggle to squeeze through. Six made it to the outer fence, but it had been prepared to keep children out as well as lions in, so they had not a hope of breaching it. As the young lions mooned about, nonplussed, between the fences movement came back to our limbs. Roger, Richard, Father and Mike leapt across the bumpy ground in great strides, as though wearing the proverbial seven-league boots, and I followed as fast as my slighter frame would allow.

Father is no whispering baritone and his staccato instructions could probably be heard in the village a mile away. In an instant, or so it seemed, wire cutters had been fetched and an opening had been cut in the inner fence. I slipped through, and, with the men covering me with their guns and whips in case of mishap, I scolded and retrieved the would-be Houdinis one by one. It was all in the day's work . . . the sort of miscalculation that is almost inevitable in any venture for which there is no precedent. There were a few strangers in the area but none had been even mildly frightened.

There was plenty of time to put matters right before the official opening. After they had been fed in the open, we rounded up the two score and ten royal beasts as easily as if they had been sheep and locked them up again for the night. A lion with a full belly is generally as placid an animal as you can meet and all they want to do after a good meal is have a snooze.

The experiment had so far been an almost unqualified success. The fence was a minor matter. Animated by victory, we all headed back to The Pheasantry for tea (the others) and coffee (me), cheerfully discussing how well things were working out.

Cook met me at the door. Marquis had been whining and pining all afternoon, she said, reproachfully. Normally, even with horses to ride and the Longleat lions to visit most afternoons I would pop in and out to see him every hour or so. Today, I had been away for hours and he did not like it. But I soon had the little five-week-old fellow in my lap, lying on his back having his belly tickled. His forgiveness was instant and sweet.

It was still a glorious afternoon and, as we sat in the wide-windowed lounge chatting away happily, as families do, I looked out on a peaceful and normal prospect in which Kumar was investigating a fat worm he had dug up, and the chimp was perched on the garden fence, drawing back his lips in a smile and making rude gestures towards us. The tenseness of the day, which we had disregarded in the excitement of the adventure, but which had hit us when it was over, was oozing out of our limbs. We fell into the relaxation of silence and the satisfaction of a job well done.

Just then the telephone switchboard blipped in the office. It was my teenage sister, Margaret, phoning from Southampton. 'Guess what!' she enthused. 'You've made the front pages of the evening papers.'

I was stunned. I had no idea that the press had been present. Roger, seeing my anxious look, had picked up an extension instrument. Margaret repeated what she had told me.

'What do they say?' asked Roger.

'Above a four-column picture of what seems to be a lion outside the fence, there's a headline about an inch deep announcing, "This Lion Escaped Today At Longleat",' said Margaret cheerily.

B

'God!' said Roger. 'We'll be for it tomorrow,' and he went through to tell my father. Release day had been solely for our experience and benefit. Care had been taken to keep the date secret. We had thought the camera-armed nosy parkers outside the reserve had been the normal daily quota of onlookers we had been experiencing for some time, but obviously at least one trespasser had been from a newspaper. Father was far from pleased, but there was nothing we could do about it except await developments.

Sure enough, the telephone shrilled many times late into the night with enquiries from national papers.

Morning brought an upsetting and erroneous story in the *Daily Express* headlined: LORD BATH'S LION CUBS ESCAPE. And we were not made less calm by a phone call from my uncle Dick Chipperfield, who was touring South Africa with the family circus. 'There's a frightening story here that eight of your lions have escaped and are roaming Wiltshire,' he said. 'Is it true?' We reassured him but it was not at all funny.

Before breakfast the first of a stream of vehicles arrived bearing photographers, TV crews and reporters, all hell-bent on finding us out at last. The more we told them that the lions were back in their cages, that there had been no danger or panic, and that all the animals and people were accounted for, the more they cross-questioned us. Were we sure? Could not a little lion have got away among so many? Could we count again?

The 'suspect' 3,200-yard perimeter double fence was examined for flaws and was photographed from every angle. It had been a main focus for criticism since the first announcements of a year before. There were now menacing hints (of the 'I told you so' variety) that we might have been negligent in its planning and construction. Nothing could have been further from the truth. My father, one of the most knowledgeable people in the world in such matters, had envisaged and created a more secure double fence than could be found anywhere.

The outer fence, of the same tough chain-link pattern as is used at most zoos, rose to a height of thirteen feet ten inches, including a two feet six reverse overhang. The inner fence (of simpler barbed-wire construction and spaced twelve feet from the outer one) was seven feet high, with an electrified 'keep off' strand at nose-height to a fully-grown lion. We were fully aware that small lions could squeeze under the inner fence, but regarded this as a simple way for them to avoid fights with their larger brethren, without causing danger to anyone.

The twelve foot safety area between the fences meant that no lion could do a proper leap at the outer fence in an attempt to escape. And, incidentally, there were constant patrols on horseback around the outer perimeter so that no children could stick their fingers through the outer fence, and so that no vandals could foolishly attempt to break in, as had been suggested.

Not that any lion *could* jump the thirteen foot ten inch outer fence (even disregarding the inward overhang). There had been much correspondence in the press about this. Actors fresh from their 'experience' in the film, *Born Free*, had assured *Daily Express* readers that they had seen lions jump or climb out of compounds surrounded by twelve feet of wire; thirty representatives from seven surrounding councils had taken this matter up; reassurances had been given by an expert from the North of England Zoological Society and from an ex-director of Uganda National Park that no well-fed lion could possibly tackle even a straight ten foot fence . . . and so on.

Throughout it all my father, quietly playing a straight bat, had stoically assured everyone that his fences were 100 per cent safe and that the reserve was more secure than a secret missile base.

Now the 'scare' stories, ridiculously blown up by the newspapers and exaggerated by our critics, were being put to the test. We patiently stonewalled all day, gradually wore down the apparently thirsty-for-blood news hounds, and hoped for a more accurate account in the follow-up stories.

There was no danger at all in the reserve. The real danger was that—as Lord Bath was forced to point out to the proprietor of a national paper which had luridly mis-stated the facts—'when the whole of this lion project has been an uphill

battle for 18 months, in which time I have personally invested over £30,000, statements such as this might easily sway
public opinion at Ministerial level against the whole project.'

With the opening less than three weeks away, this was certainly a major worry for us too, Father having invested penny
for penny with the Marquess. Various opponents of the project had indeed been inviting Mr Richard Crossman, Minister
of Housing (there being to date no Minister for Lions!) to
intervene.

So although it was unnecessary from the safety point of
view, Father announced that he would close the 'freedom
gap' for young lions by adding five feet of chain-link to the
inner fence. As far as we were concerned there were advan-
tages and disadvantages to this. The younger lions would have
to be watched more carefully in case of attack by their
seniors, but it would no longer be necessary to patrol the
outer perimeter, because there would never be lions between
the fences any more.

The wearisome and worrying day after 'release day' ended
with a visit to The Pheasantry by Inspector M. Hayward and
Sergeant B. Wakeley, of Warminster police. They were very
polite and said it was a routine, friendly visit; but the under-
lying threat of mounting opposition seemed to us to be
behind everything that was happening. Their brief was 'to
obtain names, addresses and phone numbers of people who
should be contacted in the case of certain unspecified eventu-
alities.' They emphasized that they were 'not looking at
security matters' and appeared satisfied at the information we
gave them.

Despite the substantial invasion by the press and television, and the 'jaw-jaw' that had gone on all that Tuesday,
the follow-up stories came to very little. Having found neg-
ligible substance in the 'scare' many of the papers ignored
the explanatory follow-up story. 'Lions almost eat people' is
news. 'Lions cannot possibly eat people' is not news.

The chief consolation from the event was that the earlier
story had gone round the world. At least they (the communications media) were talking about us, even if they got their
facts wrong. Longleat's lions were firmly on the map. Curi-

osity-seekers were multiplying daily and it seemed as if we would have spectacular attendances from Easter, whatever people's motives might be. It was up to us to see that every visitor got satisfaction and no lion got indigestion from eating people.

Chapter Seven

A LION LOOKS AT A LORD

A few days after the post 'release day' episode, I took the now robust seven-week-old Marquis to see his stately home and his aristocratic namesake, Henry Frederick Thynne, Knight of the Garter, sixth Marquess of Bath. As crocodiles of schoolchildren and coachloads of adults queued to pay their five shillings to tour the superb Elizabethan house, we were received in the splendid Green Library at Longleat, with its £2,000,000 collection of thirty thousand books, thought by some to be the finest in private hands in England.

An oil painting of a lion sinking its fangs into a human throat stared down at us from the wall, rather inappropriately.

The lord and the lion looked at each other steadily for a few minutes and then politely shook hands. The Marquess, in his accustomed well-worn, broad-check tweed jacket and corduroy trousers, sat in a splendid leather armchair and young Marquis squatted happily, as of the manner born, on an excellent field of Persian carpet—a lion couchant, as they say—not in the least overcome by the nobility of his host or the antiquity of the room.

'He certainly seems to be growing into a marvellous specimen,' Lord Bath ruminated amiably (having previously met Marquis at The Pheasantry in his more delicate days). 'But I must confess they're like Chinamen to me. I can't tell one from another, size for size!' We talked for a while about the forthcoming official Press Day and then I took my leave before the little lion was forced to blot his escutcheon.

I had fitted a blue leather collar to Marquis's growing neck, and I walked him back to The Pheasantry on a lead for the first time, through the heart of the magnificent 650-acre estate.

Although lions are not as happy on the lead as dogs, the collar makes them easier to handle around the house.

We gambolled past greenhouses aglow with rainbows of tulips and the warming wonder of hothouse plants, skirted the lake and took to a path in the park leading towards home. Spring was somewhat tardy; there were still a few snowdrops and crocuses in flower, in company with marsh marigolds, early violets and primroses.

The birds, wayward as always, had largely disregarded the weather. Young rooks were hatching near the big house and some baby blackbirds had already appeared, although many of their kind were still building their nests. Lapwings had produced eggs, as had a woodcock I noted (before Marquis did) among dead oak leaves, her mottled browns almost invisible, even at a few yards' range.

We had not gone far before Marquis, loping along happily, spotted a little rabbit, about the same age, I should judge, as himself. It was an irresistible occasion—two babies meeting who were almost as foreign to each other as any babies could be.

Marquis's sea-shell ears shot forward in apparent terror and his spiky whiskers bristled. The rabbit stopped more or less in mid-spring, its big eyes liquid and bemused, almost as if it was being stared-out by a stoat.

They were about a yard apart. I slackened the lead to see what action would develop. For a whole long minute they stared at each other, the African lion and the English rabbit. Then Marquis broke the spell in an embarrassingly ignoble manner. He gave a little yelp and scampered behind me for safety.

I suppose size had something to do with his reaction. All the animals at home were several times bigger. This tiny creature was smaller than his paw. Whatever the reason, it was an undignified performance for a prince of beasts who had just looked on a marquess.

As Marquis moved, the baby rabbit, released from the lion's stare of fear, resumed its stride and bounded like a firecracker across the meadow. Marquis's little paws had become glued to the ground and I was forced to carry him for a bit before he would resume his uneven jog-trot on the lead.

When he was apparently recovered in locomotion we headed for The Pheasantry with all speed, avoiding Pets' Corner (where Marquis would soon be expected to make appearances), the Fairyland Garden and the Children's Amusement Centre. Enough was enough. One encounter with the local wild life was sufficient for my African baby on his first expedition into the free green world.

Yula was waiting anxiously in the yard for our return and immediately took custody of Marquis. Off they went into a quiet corner of the office, where she fussed him and let him know how pleased she was to have him back safely, while he no doubt communicated his adventures to her.

It was fascinating that although four other orphan cubs had been introduced to the household in the past few weeks, and she was tolerant with them—allowing them to bite and wrestle with her to their hearts' content—Marquis was her darling and she still spent hours every day sleeping with him and licking his still-spotted coat until it shone with health.

Mind you, I agreed with her that Marquis was outstanding —superior in every way to any cub I had ever handled. Even at seven weeks, there was a natural dignity and intelligent charm about him I had never found in any other young animal. Proud and aristocratic dandy though he was (and he knew it) he also had that rare quality, the 'common touch'. He was sweetly biddable, amenable to suggestions and obligingly friendly with everyone—animal or human. There was no indecent haste when visitors arrived at the house. While the others would scamper around, sniffing and biting at the strange feet, Marquis would yawn, stretch himself and walk over, smiling a welcome, expressing pleasure in a purr, ready to have his paw shaken or be patted on the head—remarkable traits in one so young. In repose, too, he was a beautiful, relaxed, fairy-tale little fellow. He even smelled differently from his kin—a sort of scent of honey.

The other four were less predictable, less lovable and more true to type. Young lions generally resemble dogs much more than they do cats in their behaviour. They have few feline attributes. They are invarably brash, tough and hooligan at heart. They play rough and like to be treated that way in return.

Major, the one who could do no wrong in Roger's eyes, was the daredevil reconnaissance officer of the pets. The others would always push him off to reconnoitre anything they regarded as suspicious. He was also the pioneer in establishing new ways of tormenting the staff. His teeth were unusually sharp and he had already cultivated an individual style in infantile snarls and growls, following which he would look quizzically to see if visitors were afraid of his voice. Major would obviously be a giant and a leader when he was old enough to join a pride.

Lisa by contrast was tiny—a wispy imp of mischief, as way-ward as a squib, an active forager who lived on thrills and provoked adventure; quick-limbed and agile, she could climb the curtains in the lounge faster than any of them. The problem was that she hated turning round for the descent and would yowl from the ceiling until someone rescued her. There was a reek of cordite about Lisa and a hint of hoodoo. More than any of the others, she had to be watched for the explosion of her latent threats of anarchy.

Sheba was very much the 'loner' of the tribe—cool as they come; watchful and reserved; lean and sinewy; fragile in a beautiful way. Solitary in her habits, she was often left to her own devices but liked life this way. Feather-soft and fast in her movements, she was always the least likely to be trodden on.

Simba was handsome, bony, and bright as a knife. Quite without fear, he would get lost somewhere in the house almost daily and would return to give the impression to the others that he had secret friends he visited when he got bored with them.

The five of them played together very well on the whole, although they were as different as notes in the scale.

Larry, the pale and downy lamb, became the butt for all

the lions. When the sheep had been moved from the area marked out for the game reserve, one or two had become unsettled for a time and Larry, the first of the spring lambs that year, had been brought to me for bottle-rearing. He was such a pet that we gave him the run of the house with the others. He was totally unafraid of his lion friends, although they treated him cruelly. The trouble with Larry was that he had much longer legs than the others and was none too steady on them. So a favourite game was 'knock Larry over'. The mischievous poker-tailed cubs would take turns of charging him and sending him flying, like a skittle—a performance that would be repeated endlessly, as soon as he was up on his spindles again.

Other than this daily frolic of which they never seemed to tire, tug-of-war was the favourite sport among the animals generally. A bicycle tyre and a short length of plastic hosing were used by dogs and lions alike as tests of their strength. Surprise was an ever-present element in the tug-of-war game. A big strong dog would be chewing at the tyre or the hose when one of the cubs would sneak up on him and try to snatch it away. Or maybe there would be four or five lions tugging in something like unison at the rubber ring, trying to get it away from a dog or from Kumar, the tiger.

Stalking games were also much favoured, and often adults were the quarry. As with children, it was necessary to feign surprise when a little lion suddenly pounced, having stalked you from room to room. According to the amount of surprise shown, so the reaction of delight on the cub's face would increase.

A favourite toy which always brought purrs of pleasure was a ball I knitted for them with a bell inside; retrieving was the best fun with this. I would throw it across a room and the resultant scampering by five furry bundles could be a riot.

I have heard of people giving pets foam rubber to tear and play with, but I am emphatically against this as they can easily choke on a small piece. I learned to be careful even with the cotton wool I sometimes used to wipe their mouths. Major got hold of a piece and ate it one day. It stuck in his windpipe and he was nearly blue in the face before we got it free. I suspected that, although we had cleared his breathing, he might also have swallowed some of the cotton wool and as it could have swollen in his stomach, I watched his stool for ages. Eventually it came out three weeks later and he was none the worse.

With so many cubs about the house, keeping doors shut had to be a major preoccupation. Inevitably, this drill was sometimes forgotten, and it was always best to switch the light on in the downstairs loo before sitting down, in case you were sharing the cramped space with a playful lion or with the larger bulk of Kumar.

The lion cubs also loved scampering upstairs but hated coming down again because it was difficult and frightened them. As this reluctance to descend could result in 'accidents' in the upstairs rooms, it was always necessary to count them hastily and run to the rescue if necessary after the office or lounge door had been left open. Yula soon got to know the drill and would bound upstairs, to descend in a moment carrying a cub in her mouth.

One of the troubles in this connection—and it also applied to escape through the french windows of the office or the lounge—was that the four-month-old tiger had now learned how to open doors. When he was loose with the cubs we all had to bear his trick in mind.

Like most children, the animals did their best to put off bedtime. Able to see in the dark, they also ran much faster than any of us. As often as not, we had to bribe them into bed with their favourite toys. None of our babies was spoiled, and rough smacking was administered in the case of stubbornness or excessive naughtiness. Need I say that at the end of each day I was invariably in a condition of extreme exhaustion. But night-time bottle-feeding, plus the morning sickness I was now experiencing, still had to be faced, whatever the day had been like.

Chapter Eight

KILLERS AT LONGLEAT

March in England had come in with a wildness of lions and was going out with a meekness of lambs. At Longleat both were settling in while the spring sun beamed a welcome—the lions and the lambs. The former were being released daily to work out their problems in the 100-acre reserve. The latter were arriving all the time in other parts of the 650 acres around it.

The African lions mainly ignored the Wiltshire animals and vice versa. Cows grazed peaceably a yard or two from the perimeter fence; deer flitted and fed among the nearby oaks, elms and beeches; pheasants came and went as they pleased; hares showed their tails to the lions with cocky indifference.

This was no surprise. In Africa, animals and birds which have every reason to fear death by lion will feed and sup water unconcernedly in the vicinity of a well-fed pride. It takes but a glance for them to recognize the lethargy a full belly brings to beasts of prey.

The new 'royal' residents, in what had previously been part of the famous Longleat deer park, were having more than enough food for their needs, regularly and 'on a plate', so to speak. Lazy by nature, they were happy to rest after meals and posed no threat to anything or anyone as long as they were not interfered with.

It was their attitudes to each other that were causing us concern at this stage. We had carefully chosen the fifty individual beasts for their apparently equable temperaments, youthful vigour and good looks. There were no 'killers', no 'black dwarfs', kinky introverts or otherwise maladjusted lions amongst them as far as we could judge. They were good mixed breeding stock. And a predominance of males over females had been decided upon to avoid the risks of feline jealousies.

Three main groups of apparently well-suited animals had been carefully assembled during their six-months' quarantine on the south coast, and also during the settling-in period in the caged areas next to the huts in the reserve. This had been done in the hope that ready-made prides would divide up the park naturally into territories on release.

There had had to be a degree of guesswork about this family grouping process, because we were mixing together animals which had previously lived in places as far apart as Entebbe and Heidelberg, Nairobi and Rotterdam, Jerusalem and Hanover, Barcelona and Brussels. Most of them were young enough, we thought, to adapt. But there was no precedent to go by. No reserve like Longleat had previously been attempted outside Africa. The lions would obviously have the last word on whether they were prepared to accept our arranged marriages when living free in the reserve.

After the fence incident on 'release day', and the press invasion the day after, things settled down and the few days that followed were fairly stable. There was a certain amount of restlessness, but in the main members of individual prides stuck together while they explored the park, tentatively licked the spiky young grass and sharpened their claws on the trees. Then, having satisfied themselves that there were lots of exciting possibilities in their new way of life, and having assured themselves that full board was included in the deal, some lions began sizing up the lionesses they had not met before, rather like farmers at a market.

'Pride' is a fairly loose term used to describe the living together en famille of more than two lions. Male lions are polygamous and often group together with several females of the same family. Prides of lions in the wild usually consist of a patriarchal, fully grown male (aged anything from four to twenty years) together with a number of females, cubs and young lions of both sexes aged up to about three. Lions are considered sexually mature at about two years of age, although not fully grown until about twice that age.

The lion himself is not a good father and generally leaves the bringing up of the cubs to the females in the pride, confining his interest in them to an occasional swipe if they annoy him; and so powerful are his paw-blows that this chastisement can sometimes be fatal.

Lioness sisters frequently help each other in the rearing and training of their cubs, often remaining together in this way for many years. Lionesses come into season about every three weeks and the period of gestation is from 108-112 days. 'Father' will remain with the lioness during her pregnancy, generally looking after her a short distance away from the rest of the pride; but as soon as the cubs are born he will seek out another female with whom he can repeat the process. When, as sometimes happens, two females in a pride cub simultaneously, both litters are treated as one family and are suckled indiscriminately by one mother or the other. Indeed, it is doubtful whether each lioness can eventually recognize her own young ones. The mortality rate for cubs in the wild is as high as fifty per cent in the first year and twenty-five per cent in the second. It is very exceptional for an entire litter to reach maturity.

A pride has very strong territorial instincts and soon establishes a well-defined 'manor' of its own which is jealously guarded against other lions. The 'king' of a pride will roar defiance to all would-be intruders, backing this up with action where it is necessary.

It was soon clear that there would be many changes in the domestic arrangements we had hopefully established in the Longleat game park. Ominously, animals which had lived for anything up to a year in harmony with a family group now left to team up with others they had never seen before that week. Males followed strange females about for days, weighing up their attractions from all angles as if judging finalists in a beauty contest. Females became coy or showed off their vital statistics when a new lion they fancied approached. The younger lions and lionesses tended to cluster together. It was quite an education for those of us privileged to watch.

Gradually totally new groups began to emerge from the 'all change' manoeuvring and the stronger personalities, male and female, began to assert themselves. At this stage there were signs that some of the 'swopping' would be resisted and that fights would be inevitable.

We had selected fifteen experienced wardens and patrolmen from a large number of applicants. Dressed in bush hats and khaki clothing, and carrying .309 mm. game rifles, these now had to be particularly vigilant about breaking up fighting between the animals before it became serious. They worked long hours, but could not be expected to be in the reserve at night as well. This proved to be the most difficult time, with the nocturnally orientated beasts often scheming fights during darkness. When the nightwatchman sensed trouble, he would call out the chief game warden, Mike Lockyer, and my brother, Richard, and if I was up and about feeding my cubs at The Pheasantry I would join them. Quickly arming ourselves with whips, guns and medicines, we would dash into the park in the Land-Rover, not knowing what to expect.

I was astonished as well as intrigued at this period to find lions and lionesses I had known intimately at Southampton and Plymouth acting in ways I would never have expected of them. It was very apparent that our experiment was working out in the sense that the animals were accepting the freedom of the reserve and were reverting to primitive habits and techniques they had suppressed when they were in cages.

On one or two occasions the fights had already blazed up 'to the death' before we could reach the antagonists and we were shocked to find that the law of the jungle had prevailed, resulting in the deaths of weaker specimens.

As soon as we had identified the main aggressors, Richard decided that the only way to proceed, if we were to halt the slaughter and encourage the animals to form a stable society before opening day, was to shut away the killers at night. In this way it was hoped that they could be guided into settling their differences in the daytime while wardens were at hand to keep fights to a minimum.

The evening round-up became quite a dramatic part of the day. After the killers were singled out from the remainder, it took careful and calculated strategic manoeuvring to steer them away from the cover of brambles, ditches and bogs and into the security of the locked huts. When you consider that a fully grown lion stands about three feet six at the shoulder, weighs about a quarter of a ton and measures nine to ten feet from nose to tail-tip, you will appreciate that this drill was hazardous and exhausting. A large male lion in a rage is one of the most frightening creatures in the world to handle.

To the best of our knowledge none of the fifty lions had ever eaten human flesh, but we could not be absolutely sure. We could only be watchful.

Lions rarely attack people but sometimes an accidental kill can show them that man is an easy prey and a tasty one. After this it can become a habit. A lion which once acquires a taste for humans can never be trusted and must be killed. We were determined that fresh brisket of Briton would never be on the menu in the lion park at Longleat.

Having had it brought home to us that our lions would be more primitive and potentially dangerous when free in the reserve than they had been in zoos or huts, we prepared even more stringent precautions for the protection of visitors and increased the number of warning notices. But the experience did not deter us in any way. The whole object of the experiment was to allow thousands (perhaps millions) of interested people to enjoy the exciting experience of an East African safari in a single day, at minimal expense. We were also proud to be able to promise maximum satisfaction, for an expensive air trip to Africa can lead to subsequent travel of a hundred miles or more without the visitor seeing even a single lion, whereas no lion in our park would be more than 150 yards away from motorists driving round the two miles of twisting two-lane road, with its frequent lay-bys. Many of the natural thickets had been cleared to prevent obstruction of view and the topography was not unlike that of lion country in Kenya, with its grasslands, woods, streams and hillocks. The Lions of Longleat would therefore not only be seen clearly; they would also be seen in something very close to their natural surroundings.

Feeding the lions was all-important to the success of the scheme. When they have plenty to eat, and know where the next meal is coming from, lions are generally even-tempered, lazy beasts who are content to lie about in the sun or under the trees, dividing their time between washing themselves (in the manner of domestic cats) and sleeping. Indeed, well-fed lions move around for only about four hours in every twenty-four, averaging twenty hours per day lying down.

Experimentally, we used one zebra-painted vehicle loaded with meat and a rigidly adhered-to daily feeding time. The truck would start at the gates next to our house and drive all the way round the reserve, dropping off the meat ration for each individual lion as it went. This system later had to be modified because it led to fights and because extra 'lock gates' were added, but it was breathtakingly exciting while it lasted. Often as many as twenty lions would chase the feed truck and there would be scraps over each chunk of meat as it was thrown out.

The lions are fed mainly on bullocks' heads, supplemented by cow meat, horse on the bone, offal, whole calves and occasional ewes. In addition, all the lions receive a vitamin supplement in powder form, dusted onto the meat. This is essential for correct bone growth in young animals and adds to the health of older ones. An adult lion will consume up to twenty pounds of meat a day, but for most ten pounds is sufficient. Half a bullock's head, which costs about five shillings, is ideal trouble-free food. It takes the animal some time to get the meat off the bone. Large pieces cannot be torn off and gulped, so there is little danger of digestive upsets. The brain offers good soft sustenance. And most of the bones can be safely crunched up. There is very little waste, which is also important.

One of the many criticisms levelled at us before the opening was that there would be a serious health hazard from the feeding arrangements because lions are untidy diners and do not eat up clean. This is perfectly true. In the wild it is no problem because of the curious two-way associations lions have with several other species. Vultures, for instance, can lead a hungry lion to a meal and, in return, when a lion has made a kill and has eaten his fill, the vultures will step in and clean up the bones. Hyenas and jackals, too, often follow a pride of lions in order to scavenge the remains of the carcasses. Such camp-followers are rarely attacked because of their unappetizing flesh, but any hyena that takes too many liberties is sure to come to an untimely end. Curiously, another scavenger of lions' food is the elegant and graceful Maribou stork.

In the absence of nature's arrangements, there being no equivalent scavengers in Wiltshire, we had to send a couple of trucks round after each meal to clear up the mess. But this was done thoroughly, efficiently and to the complete satisfaction of the appropriate inspectors. Also, being experienced circus people, we knew where to sell the residue of bones at seven shillings per cwt.

Lions do not need a great deal of water to drink. Although in Africa they seldom wander far from a water-hole because such places are the surest for finding easy prey (such as antelope and zebra) they can survive for several weeks solely on the liquid content of the stomachs of their kills. But there are no water problems for the lions in the Longleat reserve because they have easy access to a stream which gurgles through the park at the bottom of the wood.

Where injuries or illnesses required treatment we used tranquillizing darts, featuring a morphine derivative. 'Darting' of wild animals is a very recent technique and at first we had to use cross-bows to fire the darts! We also employed a cage-type vehicle to convey each immobilized animal to the vet. In these and many other ways we sought to create a sanctuary as attractive and efficient as any in East Africa.

As D-Day neared, the press began to become interested in us again, and local fuss-pots flapped about, engendering more and more agitation about imagined dangers. Under questioning, Lord Bath never lost his sense of humour. 'There is no law in England which prevents me keeping lions where I want to,' he insisted, and added, 'My partner, Jimmy Chipperfield, is the expert. He tells me lions are the laziest animals in the world and will be OK as long as they are fed regularly. Of course, you might get a man-eater now and then but it would soon be spotted and shot!' This was characteristically excellent copy and kept the publicity fires well stocked.

As is well-known, the English are almost unnaturally obsessed about the welfare of animals and the smaller the animal the stronger the obsession. Someone now started a hare about lions eating native game and this was one to which we could not be certain of the answers ourselves, although early signs had been reassuring. In the wild young cubs depend on lionesses in the pride for their food for the whole of the first year, or until their second teeth are fully grown. Then they start stalking lessons with the females. The instinct to hunt is seldom well-developed and the techniques of the kill have to be learned by trial and error. Often the lionesses start the cubs on killing birds and small mammals, while they watch, guide and help. There had been no sign of this happening at Longleat but, as we parried questions, we were by no means sure that such a pattern would not emerge. So we stone-walled and remained watchful.

Simultaneously, a local crank wanted assurances that all our lionesses would be put on 'the pill' so that the numbers in the park would not quickly multiply to some hundreds of lions, as had been predicted. In fact we intended that breeding should be unrestricted and we were pleased to note that it already seemed that sex was likely to be the third most important factor in the lions' lives (after food and sleep). It was very much our intention to deal in surplus lions from the park and to add fresh stock from other places from time to time to prevent in-breeding. We hoped that a splendid Longleat strain of thick-haired lions would be available to preservationists in due course through our Chipperfield animal-dealing organization. Indeed we believed wholeheartedly that the lions we were showing and rearing at Longleat were better specimens in every way than any to be seen in Africa. So it was with delight that I noticed enlarging teats and other signs of pregnancy among lionesses in the reserve.

Castration of the male lions was also suggested by some ignoramus. It can be done, but it results in the lion losing his crowning glory—his mane. I remember a circus once castrating a lion—and thereafter they had to show it as a lioness!

One of my tasks in the frantic weeks before Easter was to 'introduce' the lions to the men who would be looking after them. They may all be Chinamen to Lord Bath but ... e each one is individual in character and in looks. All the lions had been given names at birth or on arrival—and, as a family, we tend to favour the traditional circus names, such as Leo, Simba, Lisa, Khan, Pasha, etc.—but inevitably some of them acquired nicknames according to their attitudes and behaviour in the reserve. A young lion with a short tail became 'Stumpy'; one with short legs became 'E-type'; 'Chaser' and 'Sneaky' lived up to their descriptive monikers.

Khan, Abraham and Leo, on the other hand, were dignified giants who retained their proper names. Abraham, a splendid example of royal superiority, seemed as old and wise as a god. In fact, at eighteen, he was the oldest and wisest lion in the park.

My brother, Richard, became extremely friendly with a young lioness, Lisa; so much so that she travelled everywhere in his Land-Rover with him. The wardens, too, had their favourites. But they learned to treat all the beasts with firm and friendly understanding. Lions like to look up to and respect their human associates. They naturally prefer kindly discipline to sloppy sentimentality.

Chapter Nine

MEANWHILE, BACK IN THE
ORPHANAGE...

By this time the elastic-sided office in the dining-room at The Pheasantry was bulging with desks, filing cabinets, a complicated switchboard and other equipment; and all the cupboards in the house had acquired their quotas of shotguns, big-game rifles, whips, sticks, cross-bows, darts, bullets, cartridges, antiseptics, tranquillizers, knock-out drops, snake-bite anti-serums, wound ointments, sedative solutions, surgical soaps, feeds, vitamins, clippers, worming powders, and the rest of the paraphernalia of a 'first-aid post in the wild'.

Roger, my husband, who manages the reserve, is a marvellous administrator, so it was not long before a sweet orderliness was imposed on the chaos that had threatened to result from the rest of us trying to do too much too quickly.

I should explain that my claim (which he disputes) is that I took Roger in originally as 'another stray'. He had been manager of Bertram Mills Circus at Olympia for some years at which time the Chipperfields had been rivals in circus stature as well as in the breeding, showing, buying and selling of animals. Inevitably we had met up quite often over the years, in bits of business, socializing, or to argue about this and that. So, when Bertram Mills had folded its tents forever in 1965, I felt obliged to give Roger a home. And to do so I had to marry him!

That's my story, anyway! And, for once, a stray was now more than justifying its keep!

The Pheasantry had been chosen as the commercial and human nerve-centre for the entire project, and 'nerve' was becoming the operative word.

The intention had been to have radio links from the house to the wardens and other staff. Radio telephone equipment had been ordered weeks before but had not arrived. This meant that patrol vehicles could not communicate with each other or with Roger direct; and the other employees, setting up subsidiary facilities and attractions around the park, were also out of touch. Messengers had to be used instead, so that there was a constant trudging in and out of the house by many feet. Fortunately we had contract-hired the carpet with the office equipment so it would not be *our* worry if it had to be replaced in a few weeks, as looked likely. Nor had we mentioned to the leasing firm that seven dogs would be moulting and umpteen cubs sharpening their claws around the office. They probably would not have believed us!

Anyway, as if Roger's own problems—which now also included 'front of house' preparation of publicity, advertising, tickets, posters, refreshments and souvenir sales—were not enough, I had to lumber him with the other 'orphans' quite often while I was out in the park. He then had to put up with such things as having Marquis acting as a paper-weight cum shredder, Charles (the chimp) investigating his files, and Kumar chewing his invoices . . . bearing it all with the phlegm only an ex-circus man can muster. But something had to be done to ease his situation, so a scheme of temporary restraint was worked out in which the animals would all be pilloried for several hours each day.

Cook's good nature played an important part in the plan because, in separating the cubs so that they would settle down to rest during the day and would not provoke one another to action, it was necessary to have one cub in the larder, one tied to the kitchen table and one in the passage. This meant only two of them in the office. The five accepted the situation grudgingly but without too much trouble.

In addition, Kumar was put in the garden permanently (and the lawn was abandoned for that year at least, a baby leopard I had in for training was locked in an upstairs lavatory; and I transferred my sea-lion and snake (just out of hibernation) to our Southampton zoo for the time being.

As a long-standing discipline, I always take the dogs, and any cubs or young animals I happen to have, for a walk first thing in the mornings—or rather they take me for a run. In an effort to tire them out as much as possible, I now took Marquis and the other cubs out without the dogs for as long as possible before breakfast and let them scamper around the meadows which stretch from our house almost as far as the eyes can see. I would lead them across the cattle-grid, which protects visitors to Longleat from our animal orphanage, soon after the sun came up and away they would go.

The cubs' encounters with native English wildlife in the neighbouring hedgerows and woodland margins, during those lovely spring days at the end of March and beginning of April, were great fun as well as an education in animal behaviour. Indeed these little adventures gave me almost the only periods of comparative relaxation I was able to snatch in days and nights that were becoming ever more hectic.

There are still some great natural hedges away from the main roads of Wiltshire which, for all who have the eyes to see and the ears to hear, are positively teeming with little creatures—stoat, weasel, hedgehog, brown rat, shrew, bank vole, yellow-necked mouse and dormouse, each with its individual voice and mannerisms. All that is required to observe these colonies is the animal ability to remain as still and watchful as they are.

Most mammals rely on camouflage or speed for protection and move freely only when they believe they are unobserved or alternatively when they are threatened. And to state the obvious, although they had never seen a lion cub before, the small mammals knew at once that they were in the presence of carnivores, and reacted accordingly. But the inquisitive cubs, although they could quickly flush out some lurking English furry 'beastie', were extremely naive (at that stage at any rate) and as potentially dangerous as stuffed nursery animals. Indeed, my main fear was that a rodent would be so bold one day as to bite a cub's nosy black snout. But I did not restrain them. Curiosity need not kill a healthy cat; rather it sharpens their senses and widens their experience of a not-too-friendly world.

Seven-week-old Marquis was as intrigued as the others by the creatures who lived around the estate. He would spit and snarl at the rooks which dived over him as a warning. He thoroughly enjoyed sniffing and following the spoor of animals. And he would wander happily and waywardly after a bumble-bee among the buttercups and daisies. But, unlike the other four, he would never let me out of his sight, no matter how exciting a discovery or a chase might become.

This unusual affection he offered engendered a sensuous pleasure. Dogs and horses had often had a similar regard for me in the past, but never a lion. Marquis was still a baby, of course, and there was no surety that the 'special relationship' would continue even into childhood, but I was certainly intrigued and pleased that it could be so strong. To be the one person in the life of a domestic animal is gratifying; to be similarly regarded by a horse is more rewarding; but to be exclusively respected and adored by a wild animal is the ultimate in fulfilment for an animal-lover.

I had scarcely had time up till then to realize what was happening between us and, indeed, Marquis had seen less and less of me since he had been taken off the danger list. Now I was learning daily that his special feelings had survived his period of special need and that he wanted me to know that he was tremendously glad I was his mum! That, at least,

was what he seemed to be trying to say as he returned again
and again from play to nuzzle me and rub up against me,
miaowing his pleasure at my company.

Day after day the routine would be much the same. I
would sit under a tree while the cubs chased each other
around the grasslands, or poked about under the hedges.
Marquis would keep a filial eye on me and would reap
periodic reassurances that he was all right and I was all right.
A nudge or two between us could be full of meaning, and I
would tickle his ears and send him off again with a playful
smack on his Crombie-quality coat.

In the interim, it was absolute heaven to be able to sit and
vegetate for an hour or so, maybe idly watching a grey
squirrel move stealthily among the new shoots of a beech
tree's branches; maybe listening to finches piping in the may;
maybe sniffing Jack-by-the-hedge and Ramson's garlic amidst
the thick carpet of ground ivy on which I was.

If only life could go on being as calm, simple and uncomplicated as this, I would sigh, as I rounded up the cubs and
let them pull me on their leads back to the problems of the
so-soon-to-be-opened East African Game Reserve.

Chapter Ten

FREE-RANGE LIONS

Press Day for the Lions of Longleat, to give the reserve its
official title, was 3 April, 1966, two days before it was to be
opened to the public for the first time and a week before the
Easter holiday.

Breakfast at The Pheasantry, with the entire family assembled, was a period of painful pregnant silence. Richard
was being studiously nonchalant; my other brother and
sister were pretending not to be there; Mother was unusually
subdued, and Roger was busying himself with some accounts
as he ate. I watched Father's face anxiously, to see if he was

as scared as I was, but he was giving little away—wearing his inscrutable, unapproachable look. Only his occasionally tense hands suggested unease.

This was make-or-break day in a project he had talked about for nearly as long as I could remember. Everything, miraculously, was ready in time, but there was £100,000 locked up in the scheme and overheads were eating away another £1,000 per week. On the financial score alone he had every reason for deep anxiety, although he is in every way the bravest man I know.

It was impossible then to assess the scale of his fears for the outcome. But later in the day, when all was safely realized, he was to relax and confess to a friend, 'Last night and this morning it all suddenly hit me and I was probably the most worried man in England. Although I tried to hide my feelings from the family, I knew I was reaching zero hour in the most important day of my life so far—the day towards which I had steered my scheme for nearly two years. It was either going to blow up into a nightmare or become the fulfilment of a dream. Either way there was no turning back.

'Perhaps the biggest anxiety in my mind was the fact that I was kicking against the pricks and taking on the professional animal establishment. Almost without exception, my friends had thought my idea unworkable. Many people had openly expressed severe disapproval, including some of the most respected men and women in the zoo world. Even experienced showmen had their doubts about the money-making potential of the venture. Only my immediate family and Lord Bath—God bless them—shared my confidence.

'My thoughts as I lay awake all last night ran around every sort of unforeseen and imponderable disaster. What if the lions attacked and damaged the press cars? What if a journalist or photographer or warden was mauled or killed? What if anything horrible happened to Lord Bath? What if a lion or lions escaped? What if the prides started a major fight again? It was awful. And there were no successful precedents from which I could take comfort. I was out on a limb and had to go on . . .'

As we gave up the pantomime of breakfast, leaving much

of the food uneaten, all this was before us, like a huge menacing question mark. The next few hours would give the answer to whether the park would be a pot of gold or a keg of gunpowder. The many months of sniping, knocking criticism by newspapers, officials and busy-bodies were over. Today we would see who was right.

Encouragingly, Hermann Ruhe joined us after breakfast, having flown in from Germany to give moral support. Herr Ruhe, director of Hanover Zoo and a world authority on wild animals, had been almost alone in his support for Father's scheme from its earliest day.

The animals were ready. There had been no fights for almost a week. They were in robust health—plumper and sleeker than any I had seen anywhere in the world. The staff, too, had settled in well, and rehearsals we had had on the previous few days had gone smoothly. A perfectionist by nature, Father had checked and re-checked every detail lest the press should chide us for any minor deficiency, such as an overlooked scatter of litter or a scratch on the wing of a truck.

We had prayed for a continuation of the good weather we had been enjoying but instead it had turned out to be a cold, damp, unpleasant morning. Just after nine thirty, we set off for the park, leaving an unusually nervous Roger to cope with emergencies in the office. The switchboard was flashing constantly as newspapers throughout the world checked on information, arrangements and deadlines.

Richard had preceded us and was getting a big group of lions together near the entrance gates to give a dramatic impression when the pressmen arrived. This was proving rather tricky but no sooner had we joined in the round-up than a message came through from Mike Lockyer that he was in real trouble—suddenly faced with breaking up a serious lion hunt in Born Free Valley at the other end of the reserve. We rushed to his aid. This eleventh hour disaster had blown up in an instant without any warning. The lions were once again demonstrating their unpredictability.

Apparently three big lions, who had seemed perfectly settled the night before, had chosen this ill-timed moment to settle a grudge they had with Atlas, a solitary, middle-aged, black-maned lion who normally lived near the last hut by the exit gate. Now the three were stalking him purposefully through the boggy part of the valley, with the chief game warden in hot pursuit.

Mike had just parried their attack twice when we got there and was about to drive off the marauders when his tractor got stuck in the mud. We leaped out of our Land-Rover and went to his aid on foot. There was no time for the niceties of protected vehicular pursuit.

But before we had ploughed our way through to the remote hillock where Atlas had now been cornered, a wild snarling battle was under way. Using sticks and whips we managed to scare off the three antagonists and the wardens were able to drive them into a hut and lock them up.

Atlas had put up a good show of defiance but he was quite severely injured in the process and the trees were splashed with his blood.

There was no time to reflect that this was an ominous prologue to the main performance. While we hastily got down to clearing up the mess, Father whistled up a cross-bow and 'darted' the wounded giant. It was now about ten o'clock and there was not a moment to lose. Mike quickly brought the cage-truck as near to the muddy bloody scene as he could and the now tranquilized Atlas was carted off to the vet. There would be only forty-six lions for the press to see instead of the publicized fifty, but we kept our fingers crossed that the press would run true to form and get its figures wrong.

The press coaches and cars were expected within half an hour, so we all hurried back to The Pheasantry to tidy up our clothes and change our boots. Fortunately for us, there was no time to pause and think of the implications of the fight. Whatever had happened, we must not be late for the opening ceremony, and the chances were that Lord Bath and his press officer, Andrew Bowen, would already be in place finalizing the speeches.

I had even less time than the others because this was to be Marquis's big day as well as ours. In the strain of the morning I had failed to feed him and he now let me know in no uncertain fashion with a light shower of uncharacteristic spitting plus a yowl reminiscent of a tomcat on the tiles. I hastily fed him (while Roger attended to the other equally hungry cubs between phone calls) and put on his best Sunday-go-to-meeting blue leather collar. The others had left by then, so I hopped into the nearest car and, with Marquis perched in the passenger seat for his very first chauffeured ride, drove at full belt to where the journalists were assembling around the official rostrum—an open truck. It was about one minute before scheduled 'opening time'—ten thirty a.m. I handed Marquis, plump as a plum from his feed, to the Marquess and the little lion at once rudely inaugurated the proceedings, to everyone's delight, with a post-breakfast belch.

'This, gentlemen, is a lion, albeit a naughty one,' Lord Bath announced amiably.

'Looks more like a leopard,' someone responded, which was true enough for the uninitiated. All lion cubs have spots and Marquis's were more pronounced than most.

The Marquess went on to explain that Marquis was the first Lion of Longleat and the only one they would be able to interview or handle. 'The others may look tame but they are in truth unpredictable,' he went on, not knowing that four of them had so recently proved his point.

Representatives were present from every English national newspaper, from four TV companies, from magazines, provincial and foreign papers and newsreels. Inevitably, they all wanted to hold Marquis and he did not mind the attention in the slightest. They lionized him and in return he humanized the most cynical of them as he showed off all his tricks. I was a little afraid of the effect the flash-bulbs would have on him. At first the lights made his eyes flash like signals on a pin-table, but I assured him in a quiet voice that it was nothing to be afraid of and he went on hamming away like a precocious performing kid.

When the first wave of picture-taking was over, Lord Bath —wearing a safari hat and a red-spotted tie—plunged into his main speech, sparkling and provocative as ever.

'History is in the making today,' he said. 'My namesake is of the species *panthera leo*. You will shortly meet many more of his kind roaming free in the wilds of Longleat. I have introduced *panthera leo* partly to counter *anobium tessellatum* —the death-watch beetles that nibble away thousands of pounds worth of my beloved ancestral home every year.

'When we move among the lions you will be in no danger as long as you stick to the rules and remain in your cars. I have met most of them in the past few months and you have my assurance that they are frightfully docile and absolutely charming.

'There was one nasty one,' his lordship went on cheerfully, 'but we got rid of him. I've got three *rampant* lions on my coat-of-arms, but the ones you will be seeing out there are all *couchant*. You'll even see them being fed. Normally this happens only six days a week (and never on the sabbath) but we've decided to give them a Sunday joint in your honour. I suppose the six-day rule is a throw-back to the days when they ate Christians once a week, but I'm having none of that here.

'People put me down as a bit mad,' he went on, 'but the situation is simply that I love this place so much that— although I'm basically shy—I force myself to do things to attract people to Longleat and so make money to preserve it. However, I'm not a stunt man. There are limits to what I'll do for publicity. Everything must be dignified. I'm not running a circus, like the Duke of Bedford; and I'm not running a garage like Lord Montagu (whose actual house is only a cottage beside mine).

'This is a very serious and important day for me. I'll be disillusioned with nature and with nature lovers if the lions do not lure in at least 100,000 additional visitors a year. I also hope the lions will breed prolifically enough not only to perpetuate the local species but to make a side profit in sales to zoos, circuses and even to rival African reserves.

'I have had to overcome many local apprehensions, but they were mainly my own fault. What went wrong was that I got a bit tight and announced the scheme prematurely. In fact, although cars and people are fully covered by insurance, up to £100,000, the park is as safe as houses. Our peacocks are more liable to do damage than Mr Chipperfield's lions. Sunshine brings the peacocks and peahens down from their resting places in trees and walls. They tend to land on glossy car bonnets, see their reflections and peck merrily away with their beaks. Nor are they as melodic and tuneful as our lions, which, as you can hear, give out a friendly roar of welcome— a roar more soothing than frightening. The peacocks, on the other hand, make an unearthly, unfriendly screeching noise. I'm all for having lions around the place.'

And he concluded, 'You will be given sticker discs for your cars (as will the public) proclaiming "I have seen the Lions of Longleat." I asked the artist who painted the illustration for it to depict a particularly benevolent lion, like the M.G.M. lion, you know, that looks as though it's yawning rather than roaring!'

In a short and impressive speech, Herr Ruhe told reporters, 'This is a very important occasion for preservationists. You are honoured to be present at the launching of the only place outside Africa where one can move about freely among lions living in their natural state.'

And Father, equally briefly and to the point, told the newsmen, 'Apart from the novelty, this is a serious project in the study of lions and the way they live. We shall soon know many things about them we have never known before.'

The hundred or so newsmen were then led on a fifty-minute safari through the reserve by Lord Bath, with the quip, 'Come and see my free-range lions.' Astonishingly, the entire scene was idyllically peaceful. The prides were acting like respectable families on a Sunday afternoon picnic. Solitary animals were taking an after-lunch nap on the verandahs of their insulated shelters. They had never had it so good. My horses, which were being ridden around the perimeter, showed no disturbance when they scented lion. The neighbourhood cows, far from losing their milk yield, had to be prevented from pressing their noses against the chain fencing as they ruminatively inspected the lions. A children's riding class passed safely along an estate path. And sheep did safely graze.

As had been planned, I brought Lisa forward when we reached her—a ten-month-old quiet and friendly Dublin Zoo-reared lioness I had trained. She dutifully licked the Marquess's hand with her rasping tongue, while the flash-bulbs popped. 'I should not be doing this,' said Lord Bath jovially. 'It's against my own rules, but it's fun.'

In all, thousands of photographs were taken plus miles of film. As the cavalcade moved around the metalled road, one of the lionesses who was in whelp unpredictably lunged at a car and scratched a side panel. That was all. The others behaved impeccably.

The greatest excitement was when a golden pheasant momentarily alighted on Abraham's back and was totally ignored by the old lion. The pheasant then pecked at Abraham's mane, presumably looking for ticks, and still got no response, so it spread its wings in a leisurely way and flew off . . . whereupon my grip on Marquis's collar slackened and he gulped a cry. I had all but strangled my friend in the tension of the moment.

We had been unable to sleep the night before for worrying about the imponderables. Now, with press day successfully surmounted, there were the newspaper slants to lose sleep over. Where it had not mattered much what they said earlier, as long as they mentioned the Longleat project, it was now very important that we should reap a good press.

There was no need to worry. The next day we had acres of coverage—all of it, praise be, favourable, except that Marcus Lipton, MP, had suddenly decided to get in on the act and was trumpeting woe to all who visited Longleat. He had less support, however, than Jeremiah in the wilderness, and it was abundantly clear we had it made, as they say.

We sat in the sitting-room and out-shouted each other, as we picked up paper after paper, until the pets and cubs thought we had all gone mad. It was a press officer's dream. If we had had to pay for the hundreds of column inches we achieved across the world, in news comments and pictures, it would have cost more than Marquis's weight in gold.

Even *The Times* was forgivably amiable. In a prominent story (accompanied by a picture eleven inches deep, over three columns) it said the following:

Nobody was eaten here today. The first safari into the lions' compound was watched with disdain by all of the lions in the pride except two.

Espying a cavalcade of none too tasty-looking journalists, a lioness crouched menacingly, glared like a politician given an awkward question, and ran at a car. At the last moment the lioness swerved, barging it with her shoulder, and loped off.

The only other real contact was when a group of cubs strolled towards a party of photographers in vehicles. Lord Bath, wearing a fetching American hat, was halfway out of his car. It looked a dangerous moment.

One of the cubs approached at a trot, a white hunter with a loaded gun stood by and Mr Richard Chipperfield, a member of the circus family, stood his guard.

The cub turned out to be one of his friends and Lord Bath stroked it bravely.

The safari had begun forebodingly enough as the party drove past a sign pointing to 'Heaven's Gate. No Coaches' . . .

. . . Outside the first entrance gate today a 'white hunter' in bush hat and khaki sat astride a horse as in an illustration from a boys' adventure story. He is one of 15 recruited with experience of big game.

There were more guards at two further gates, the second of which opens into the 97-acre compound. Inside, three marksmen, each accompanied by a driver, are on duty in Land-Rovers.

The 46 lions already here roam at will beneath the trees in the compound, laze on the verandahs of their insulated shelters (made from railway banana wagons) or pace up and down inside the fence, eyeing meaty cows in the parkland beyond. On each of six days a week every lion is thrown 14s. worth of meat.

The compound will be open to safaris by the public from Tuesday.

This was very different in every way from *The Times*'s attack of six months before. And this, more than any story, underlined the fact that we had arrived. It was as near to an apology and a salute as could be expected from an erstwhile enemy.

Lord Bath was absolutely knocked out by the press and television coverage. He was also somewhat tickled by a letter which arrived from his great rival, the Duke of Bedford. This read (in part):

My Dear Henry,

I am sure that you could put on a splendid Roman Revival scene at Longleat and throw occasional ones of your customers to the lions and that this would prove extremely popular. I should be very happy to send my Trustees along for this, as long as you did not tell them about it until they got there. It would be the most constructive thing they ever did.

Ian.

This tended to confirm my suspicions that the notorious public quarrels between the two stately homes' leaders cloaked private affection, respect and 'in' fun.

Chapter Eleven

THE BEATING-OUT OF MANY PATHS

Tuesday saw us in very different mood from Sunday. The good press was continuing, enquiries were numerous and it seemed certain the public would be beating out many paths

Keystone Press Agency

Marquis's first spring at Longleat

Suppertime

Swimming with Suki

Kumar at $2\frac{1}{2}$

Mary filming at Pinewood with the Indian pythons Hereward and Mathilda

It's a dog's life at The Pheasantry

London Express News and Feature Services

Checko, Mary and Sheila making friends on the *Dr. Doolittle*
location at Castle Coombe

Marquis and Mary, September 1967

Marquis and the mouse

Charles the
exhibitionist

Simon, Alby and Mor
repel a sea-lion from
Chimp Island

Keystone Press Agency

from all over the country to see our lions.

It had been hoped at one time that the Duke of Edinburgh would perform the opening ceremony but duties elsewhere prevented this. So it had been decided that at ten a.m. on Tuesday, 5 April, the Marquess would simply welcome the first visitors and we would then get on with the job. This he did with his usual aplomb, acting as gatekeeper and ticket-issuer for a time. And so pleased was he that he pocketed the very first pound note and later had it framed to hang in his study. He also posed tirelessly for photographs and signed autographs galore for 'I spoke to a stately lord' patrons.

Admission charges were £1 per car, irrespective of the number of occupants; 5s. per coach passenger; and 7s. 6d. for anyone choosing to be driven around in a safari vehicle.

Things went fairly smoothly at first. Admission to the main reserve was effected by passing through a small entrance enclosure, approximately a hundred yards long, fenced for the whole distance on either side and with a gate at each end. This could accommodate up to a dozen waiting vehicles and the arrangement was that when the one gate was open the other was closed. Prominent signs warned, 'You are now in lion country. Do not open your car doors or windows'; 'Do not feed the animals'; and 'If your car breaks down, sound your horn and wait for a white hunter'. Traffic was signposted to travel one-way only, with no U-turns. Loud-speaker announcements repeated all these warnings frequently in case anyone could not read.

As the amateur zoologists (with tigers in their tanks and lions in their thoughts) rolled around the twisting road, the problems of operating the park began to appear. At the out-set, communications between members of the staff operating the reserve were very obviously lacking. The failure to deliver our radio-phones meant that the drivers of the five patrolling vehicles were unable to get in direct touch with each other and with the gate staff, let along with the 'brains' at The Pheasantry. Also we found we were rather understaffed in the light of the problems and tasks that emerged in actual operation; so much so that there were insurmountable difficulties over meal breaks and knocking-off hours.

C

All in all, the 164 cars which passed through the reserve on that very first Tuesday were more than enough for us to cope with. We were now concentrating on the fact that we had only three days to prepare before the Easter weekend rush was upon us. The problems we had not thought of were being thrown up hourly, and we could have kicked ourselves for not anticipating some of them.

The crux of the matter was that we had concentrated too much on the animals and too little on the people. In the event, the lions gave the impression of being urbane and sophisticated—mainly ignoring the stream of cars in a superior sort of way—while the people seemed to be maddeningly capricious, not to say stupid. Like many a pioneer before us, we were finding out that all our simple rules had to be spelled out much more carefully and often than we had dreamed to be necessary and that every one of us had to be constantly on the alert to new and alarming facets of human behaviour for which we would have to compensate before the Easter crowds arrived. It seemed as if people were determined to be eaten by lions, the way they went on.

Above all, we had to introduce shift working for the wardens and drivers. who were in a state of high tension throughout every minute of that first long day, realizing that a moment of unwatchfulness could easily lead to a matter of life and death.

Apart from a great rash of people disobeying the signs and opening windows or doors the better to 'shoot' the lions with their cameras; vehicles breaking down in the reserve; and cars illegally back-tracking (in reverse or by U-turning) . . . there was the totally unforeseen problem of the dogs. The first we knew of it was when a breathless messenger dashed into The Pheasantry at lunchtime on the first day to say we were wanted urgently in the reserve. Richard and I got there as fast as we could, not knowing what to expect. In the event, we could hear the problem before we could see it. Somewhere among the lions a couple of small dogs were yelping as if the day of judgment had come and a hound was baying his mournful accompaniment.

The penny dropped at once. We had never thought of

people being so silly as to take their pets along for the ride and so we had not posted notices forbidding it.

So an extra man had to be posted hastily on the gate to ensure that any doggy passengers were removed before their owners' car were allowed to proceed. And a girl groom was seconded from my stables to take care of the pets until their owners returned for them.

Even so, British dog-lovers are astonishing people. There was considerable indignation when this new rule was explained to some of the pet-owners. A few turned about and went home in a huff, refusing to look at the lions if Fido could not look, too. And in other cases, especially with French poodles named Fifi, poor henpecked father would be left outside the compounds to walk the darling dog while mother drove on with the rest of the family. It was most instructive!

During the first and second day we tethered the left-behind pets along the approach fences, while workmen laboured nearby to build, before Easter, a second animal compound, as it were—a large and reasonably soundproof dog-house. This was yet another lesson learned. The noise of the barking had already begun to upset our pets (and our nerves) at The Pheasantry, apart altogether from the effect it was bound to have in the long term on animals in the park.

Another aspect of safety we had not thought of was that of soft-top roofs and open cars. These, too, had to be banned as a safety precaution. Their occupants were offered rides in safari vehicles for the same sum as they would have paid for their cars.

All too soon the Easter holidays were upon us, and what a scene that was to be! None of us, least of all Father or Lord Bath, had anticipated the immense volume of traffic which would arrive at Longleat over the long weekend.

The AA and RAC had done a good job of signposting the area and, almost from dawn on Good Friday, the various lanes that led from the main Warminster-Frome road to Longleat became jam-packed with some hundreds of cars. So sudden and unexpected was the rush that some of the later arrivals could not be processed through to the reserve in less than six hours. It was an unforgettable day of toil, sweat and tears.

Roger worked ferociously to improve the access situation but, even so, such was the invasion on the morning of Easter Sunday that soon after breakfast the queue stretched for about seven miles, right into the heart of Warminster. This was the first of the many early headaches for the local police as well as for us. Apart from the extra burden of traffic direction and control, they were besieged by calls from local residents who could not get their cars out of their garages into blocked roadways.

Churchgoers never got there. Villagers were unable to reach the local for their accustomed midday drinks. Lunches burned as housewives helped over-heated car owners of over-heated cars with buckets of water. Sunday newspapers failed to be delivered. The entire area was in chaos and we were the culprits.

Nor were things helped by teeming rain which went on all day. When the cars began to leave the reserve, and had to queue again in the single-lane park roads out of Longleat, the most incredible jam built up. Normally, some of those leaving would have parked to rest and picnic on the grassland, but conditions were so muddy that day that nobody dared leave the narrow roads. In no time at all, the straggling stream of cars had built up from the lion reserve right through to the point where the approach roads met the main road.

At one point in the afternoon, *nothing* was moving and the backlash of the queue stretched right round the winding road of the lion reserve itself.

This posed a totally new and rather frightening problem.

Some of the poor car occupants had been locked in with the lions, so to speak, for hours by now, and not a few of them were crossing their legs in anguish! This meant that Richard with his small team at one end of the reserve and Mike with his at the other were nearly at their wits' end keeping the lions at bay when people suddenly hopped out of their cars in desperation—nature's call being stronger than fear when it came to the crunch—in search of a tree behind which they could relieve themselves. One man, unable to find such a hiding place, took to his heels and ran the hundred yards or so to the exit gate, with a couple of young lions in pursuit, before anyone could get to him.

As it was very early in April, the hours of daylight were limited. The result was that, thanks to all the snarled up traffic, there was still a half-mile queue of cars waiting to get *in* to see the lions when darkness began to fall at seven p.m. And at this point the reserve itself was still jam-packed with vehicles.

There was nothing for it but to turn away those still waiting. They were none too pleased about this, some having driven hundreds of miles and waited around for hours, but we had no alternative. Our main concern was to get the visitors *out* of the lion park before it was really dark. In the latter stages of this operation, drivers began switching on their headlights in the reserve. This frightened the lions and we all had to be even more vigilant. It also frightened Roger and his gatekeepers. They were blinded by the lights and terrified lest a lion should follow a car out, unnoticed in the glare.

But it all ended happily and we slept the sleep of the tired just, secure in the stunning knowledge that at least 50,000 people had safely been out on safari among our lions.

As soon as Easter was over, and we had a moment to breathe freely, we held a conference to consider the lessons we had learned and to adopt new procedures, most of which have been in use ever since.

One of the chief of these was in the matter of car windows. Over the hectic Easter weekend examples of drivers brazenly ignoring the rules (printed on their tickets as well as being prominently displayed and often announced) had multiplied alarmingly. It is understandable that the temptation is considerable, when an apparently tame lion approaches the car, to wind down a window for a closer look or a quick photograph to show friends back home.

But my father's whole concept had been of people driving around, safe because they were mobile and because they had steel and glass between them and the lions.

The daftness of the public, in so often ignoring the warnings had frightened the staff more than anything. *They* were fully aware, even if the visitors were not, that, although ninety-nine times out of a hundred the lion would ignore the open window, there were a number of animals in the reserve whose characters were such that, if momentarily scared by something, they could leap into the opening before anyone's reflexes could close the window. The answer to this—the public being what it is—was even more vigilance and therefore still more staff.

Breakdowns had proved another major source of anxiety. None of us had envisaged there being as many as there were over Easter. Many of the cars had travelled very long distances to get to Longleat Inevitably, they chose the middle of the lion reserve finally to snuff it. There were also electrical faults; there was overheating again; there were damp distributors; there were punctures—all among the lions. Some cars even ran out of petrol in the reserve. So serious was this aspect that we found it necessary to employ a local garage to have a zebra-painted breakdown truck on constant patrol with our other vehicles. The mechanics were somewhat put out at first by the experience but soon got used to it.

In the first few days, we also found that some lions would chew at the tyres of broken-down vehicles, to the consternation of the families there, but after they had all had a nibble at the rubber, and found it unappetizing, they eventually desisted!

There were also cases of wing mirrors bitten off, and aerials broken in half, but the customers seemed more proud of their prowess than annoyed at the damage.

In the midst of all this early confusion and improvisation, Lord Bath was a cheerful and tireless tower of strength. He continued to help Roger to collect the money; he posed for more and more pictures with visitors; he flourishingly signed 'Bath' on booklets and grubby pieces of paper with the same charming smile; and he listened to as many minor complaints as the rest of us.

One way or another, 99.9 per cent of the first week's visitors were sent away happy and fulfilled and it is astonishing, in view of the unforeseen problems, that not more than half a dozen letters of complaint were sent to Longleat.

One of the oddest of these came from a man who said he had enjoyed his visit but was deeply concerned for the welfare of the lions. He felt that the exhaust fumes from the cars might be extremely harmful to them. And his positive suggestion was that we should rebuild the roads so that cars could coast down into Born Free Valley, with their engines switched off. We laughed a lot about that and it helped relieve our tensions. If he reads this, I hope the kindly gentleman will accept my assurance that not one lion has been asphyxiated in the intervening years, and not one has developed lung cancer!

There were phone calls, too. I remember one from the local police to the effect that someone had reported seeing a lion walking along the A 303 near Yeovil and was it one of ours? We said 'no' but we were just a bit anxious in case one had managed to follow a car out. A roll call showed all were present and correct. We heard no more about the Yeovil lion. Anyone seen it since?

My father is no fool. As soon as he had satisfied himself that his project was an even greater success than he had dreamed, and as soon as we had sorted out the main problems in conference, he flew off to Nairobi, leaving Richard, Roger and me in charge.

No sooner had he reached the sunshine of Kenya—on the Wednesday after Easter—than I had to telephone him to say that we had struck a new problem—snow! About twelve inches had fallen overnight and no road was available in the reserve for the few hardy visitors who wanted to drive through.

This was bad enough, but the effect on the lions was slightly traumatic. They had just been settling in nicely and were using the now-open huts less and less, preferring to settle out of doors, in their own little corners of the park. I had tramped out in my high boots that morning, half scared lest any of our lions had died of shock in the night, and had found a group of four lionesses huddled against the perimeter fence, getting what shelter they could from some bushes there. Others were squatting by the trees, looking far from happy. We rounded them all up and put them in the huts with warm, dry straw, whence they scarcely stirred during the two days the snow lasted.

The few visitors who arrived were asked to leave their cars outside and were driven around in our big caged-in lorries, to avoid disappointing them. The lions looked out at the caged people, from their cosy huts, and probably had a good laugh, but the visitors, too, seemed to enjoy the unusual experience. Actually, it should, perhaps, be noted at this point that the Lions of Longleat reserve never closes. It is open every day of the year, more or less from dawn to dusk.

Father had gone to Kenya to put in hand a big giraffe-catching expedition. 'Don't worry about the snow,' was his laconic rejoinder when I telephoned him. 'The sooner the lions learn about Wiltshire weather, the better they'll settle down. They're English now!'

Chapter Twelve

LIONS WITH SNOW ON THEIR PADS

After two days of snow there was a thaw and then the cold weather came back even worse than ever, chucking down the white stuff and very cold at nights. Frozen Wellington boots gently steaming by the fire and the trudge of workers or wardens in and out of The Pheasantry, due to the prolonged non-arrival of the radio equipment, became necessary features of mid-April, as we continued to be buried under the outflow of the lingering snow clouds of winter. This time, the animals in the park decided to investigate the phenomenon and soon were frisking around in the crisp powdered carpet, becoming whiter than the purest white hunter as they rolled in drifts or allowed a snow shower to cover them. And all the while they sensibly grew denser coats and more luxurious manes in self-defence. In fact, lions prefer snow to rain and are much more active and interesting in the cold weather.

As for the cubs and pets in the house, they just did not care a monkey's cuss about the weather. Left a lot to their own devices, they alternatively tore around getting in everyone's way or slept off their excesses in their baskets or chairs, their snores and whistles shaking the house like a roundabout getting up steam. Born free? This gang of tearaways were having the time of their young lives while the rest of us were shackled daily to mounting problems of administration and sheer hard graft.

Marquis had adopted the old rocking chair in the dining-room. It was his, and woe betide any human or animal who sat in it if he felt tired. Major good-naturedly shared a settee with Amy, the Schnauzer and Larry the lamb; Simba had his secret corner by the kitchen stove; Lisa and Sheba still favoured the baskets they had been raised in. At eight weeks, or thereabout, they had all been inoculated against feline enteritis (or cat 'flu), which is the main worry as far as raising lions is concerned, and they seemed none the worse. Their coats were becoming finer, less Teddy-bearish and more shiny, aided in Marquis's case by Yula's continuing motherly attentions. Meanwhile my other tiger, Suki, had to spend a lot of her time in the kennels with the larger dogs. She had grown the frame of a giant but still had the spirit of a child.

By now, Marquis and the original cubs had produced full sets of beautiful, sharp first-teeth. This led to two changes in routine. They began their destructive period—tearing at furnishings and biting furniture—and so had to be watched and disciplined more strictly. And they were gradually weaned off the bottle, as they were able to chew and digest meat. They began to have best mince, an occasional bone to strengthen their molars, and chopped chicken twice a week.

In an effort to use up some of their fantastic energies, I still allowed them to take me for a run, bucking and snorting in the cold, every morning, snow or no. In fact they soon came to like it, scattering white clouds behind them like toy snowploughs and shaking off the surplus on their coats in each others' faces, as they scampered around the frozen baldness of the woods, among trees creaking with the weight of snow and bristling with frozen spikes, some already lopped by their burdens of ice.

One day they came upon the corpse of a sheep buried in a snowdrift, but, whatever it meant to them, they obviously did not recognize it as frozen food and soon tired of the stiff furry object as a possible plaything, easily tempted away to a chase by a solitary squirrel darting for cover among tree roots clinging to a hillock, in a mattress of pine needles, like giant frozen hands.

Best fun for them and for me was the little kidney-shaped pond, near The Pheasantry, now as black and flat as a polished grand piano top, but normally the haunt of moorhens, dabchicks, frogs, lizards, dragonflies, reed-warblers, tiddlers, tadpoles and other delightful English water-dwellers. The African lions adored it in its frozen state. Marquis was the first to discover that he could slide, like a Mini on a skid-pan. One by one the others got the message, and from then on, every day they would charge on to the glassy tray apparently fearlessly until some mishap would bring them back to reality, with a squeal of claws or an undignified bump at the pond's edge.

I would sit, when I could, on the low branches of a willow, used as swings by children in summer, and watch little bubbles rising, like green stars, under the surface of the ice . . . until all my cubs would end up lying prone, making swimming motions on the ice, kicking and squawking until I rescued them.

Looking at their reflections, and mine, in the frozen spring water, I was reminded of the first time baby Marquis was well enough to totter about our bedroom, where he chanced to encounter my cheval mirror. It was the traditional story-book performance: the first startled, bucking reaction; the expression that said 'this is another lion but it looks like me and moves like me . . . why doesn't it smell? . . . why won't it play? . . . why is it cold and hard to touch?'

Baffled after the first encounter, Marquis had kept away from the looking-glass from that day on.

Because he slept in our bed (regarding it as his place of

safety and privilege) Marquis was usually allowed to stay up later than the other cubs and he was a pleasure to have around as we sat working at the accounts for the reserve or planning future schedules. More than any dog or other pet I had ever had, he showed his affection and sensitivity in a hundred ways in the comparative peace of the evenings. If I was under more strain than usual he would nuzzle me understandingly. If I was feeling unwell, his big eyes would look into mine anxiously. He always knew when it was good for me to play a game with him and so cheer myself up; he could sense instantly when I sat in an armchair whether I wanted him in my lap or preferred him nearby on a pouffe. The evenings, indeed, were the times of intimacy and quietude when love and trust were fostered. Although getting too old for soppiness, Marquis enjoyed most of all to doze off with my thumb in his mouth, fed, happy and loved.

Occasionally on the snowy April evenings I would take him around the reserve with me when the crowds were gone and I had to see that all was quiet. And one night, when Roger was away in Plymouth on business, I had a mad whim to get the toboggan out and hurtle down a hill slide some of the village children had been using during the day. Of course, I took Marquis. He loved being involved in any child-like activity and sledging seemed to me to be right up his boyish street.

As I dug through a great accumulation of miscellaneous rubbish in a cupboard at the back of the house, searching for the large abandoned steel-tracked sledge I had had since I was about ten, I chattered away to Marquis and he showed clearly that he was as excited as I was at the prospect of some new adventure. And in the kitchen he watched, all big-eyed and drooling, every move I made as I cleaned and polished the long-discarded sleigh.

As soon as we were out of the gate and across the cattle grid, I sat the excited little lion, now about the size of a five-year-old child, in the centre of the sledge and hauled him along the rutted tracks to the hill known as Heaven's Gate. After an initial bout of nervous wavering, Marquis sat back and enjoyed the ride, purring his pleasure.

I sat up for the first few flashing hurtles down the hill, my feet steering the sledge and Marquis clutched safely in my lap, nervously licking my face. Like a child, he was always willing to try anything, provided 'mum' was there holding him. Like a child, he soon gained confidence and, after about half a dozen upright trips, I lay prone for a faster one and he crouched on my back, clinging tight with his blunted but still discernibly gripping claws. The track was a fairly even and safe one, so we had no mishaps. We both enjoyed every moment of it, to the point that we must have made about thirty trips in all, shrieking and grunting our pleasure dementedly to each other in the otherwise deserted slopes, as we plunged breathlessly through diamond-flecked trees, all charcoal and red in the setting sun.

Tired but happy, we made our way home in the manner of our arrival, the sledge's runners sharply biting through the night's new frost, feeling a little like lost tropical hunters who had first wandered north and stumbled into the Ice Age . . . glad nobody knew of our mad frolic.

Passing the stables and kennels I called out that all was well and was answered by the rattle of chains, a pony's sigh and the gentle whine of a dog. Into the house, warm in its bed of snow, we bounded, leaving the sledge outside till morning, half-thinking that we could repeat the pleasures of the experience before the others were up . . . But life seldom works that way. Instead, in the morning the radio men arrived at last and installed a master set in the office at The Pheasantry (with out-stations all around the estate and reserve), which became a source of wonder and delight all that day to the humans and a matter of fear and conjecture for the animals, to whom Marconi's works were a hindrance rather than a help to communication. The more the receiver in the corner chattered, the less attention they received, which was, of course, the only possible way to look at the matter.

That same day, too, the snow left us for the rest of that year at least.

Chapter Thirteen

KILLERS WHO ARE OUTSIDE
THE LAW

By making such an enormous success (in terms of safety as well as of public acclaim) of the Longleat lion project, we had disappointed a lot of our critics, who had been hoping to see us fall flat on our faces. The crowds were rolling into the park again in their thousands, in perfect late-April weather, and not one little Albert had been eaten to date. It was perfectly beastly of us to have proved so many experts wrong and to have given pleasure to so many amateur animal-lovers. Indeed, some of the pundits, who sounded off so boldly in the press, will never forgive us for making fools of them.

We also opened the eyes of rival stately home owners, zoo proprietors and conservationists to the tremendous possibilities there were for such ventures all over Britain.

Some had thoughts too of re-introducing wild species once native to these islands, and I welcomed, with reservations, the airing that this fascinating idea was given. It is sobering to recall that before man eroded natural life by introducing agriculture, industry, towns, roads, reservoirs, drainage, and other sophistications, there were wild cats, lynx, beaver, bear, moose, bison, wolf and lammergeyer throughout Britain and northern Europe.

But, despite our efforts to put something back in the way of wildlife for study, enjoyment and breeding, I had my doubts about some of the suggestions that followed the news of the success of our reserve.

The idea of having wild bears prowling around the moorlands of Yorkshire and wolves roaming the Scottish highlands was a fascinating romantic notion, but impractical, it seemed to me. But it was put up in all seriousness by Mr Brunsdon Yapp. Mr Yapp's views carried some force, as he was Senior

Lecturer in Zoology at Birmingham University and a member of the National Parks Commission.

His proposal was that bears, lynxes and wolves should be re-introduced to the common lands of Britain, to roam even more free than our lions. 'There seems,' he said simply, 'to be no more danger from these animals than from the bulls we tolerate in our fields.' His reasoning was that these predators were perfectly natural hazards here not so very long ago—the bear until the days of William the Conqueror; the wolf until about 200 years ago. In his opinion, their return would cause a more favourable balance of nature by reducing the numbers of pests which are their natural prey.

As one example, he cited the highlands, 'where there are no predators, and where deer are protected from the attacks of man, so that they increase to such an extent as to overgraze their pastures and become a nuisance.' Wolves, he claimed, would put that right. Or even lions! 'A few wolves or lions,' he argued, 'would keep down the number of deer and probably increase the size of individuals by removing weaklings.' Strengthened, no doubt by the news that our lions were now largely ignoring the cars in their midst, Mr Yapp pressed home his point by insisting that the danger to humans from large carnivores has been exaggerated. 'Brown bears,' he pointed out, 'and wolves still exist in some mountainous parts of Europe, but reports of their attacks on man are seldom heard. Even in those parts of Africa where lions still exist, reports of attack on man are almost non-existent.' And he added, for good measure, the facts that the same is true of the grizzly bear (*ursus horribilis*) in American national parks and the smaller black bear which would 'soon be accepted here as a delightful tourist attraction'.

It was an interesting and provocative suggestion. But my instincts and experience reject it instantly. Bears are certainly the world's most vicious and untrustworthy animals and can cause the most terrible injuries for no apparent reason. Wolves are vicious creatures, too, and lions in the wild will kill a man if it suits their purpose at the time. Nowadays, our national parks are far too small to be used as outdoor menageries for the larger carnivores, but there may be a case for re-introducing smaller species.

A main worry in my mind at the time was that Mr Yapp's authoritative words might make people even less wary than they are of creatures of the wild. I am always most careful to point out, when showing cubs or larger animals in public, that even the most apparently tractable of them can suddenly change, for any one of a dozen reasons, and become a killer. It worries me terribly that we appear, quite unintentionally, to have inspired more and more ordinary people to keep wild animals as pets. The flood of publicity that preceded and heralded the Lions of Longleat opening now seemed to be resulting in lions being kept in London flats and suburban backyards. Maybe some of them had been there all the time, and it was through our publicity that the press began finding so many stories of private zoos and peculiar pets.

But whatever the balance of causes and effects, I have a bit of a guilt complex about the dangers people may be running, all unwittingly, because of me; and I cannot proceed with the story of Marquis and my other animals without pausing here to issue the warning that amateurs will be well advised to think twice before taking any wild creature into their homes.

The trouble partly was and is that, in the course of the controversy over our pioneering lion park, it had been revealed that no licence is necessary to buy or keep wild animals (except for great apes, rhinos, kangaroos and wallabies). And, unless they are hooved animals, or belong to the cat or dog family, they do not even have to serve a period in quarantine. You can even call your private collection a zoo and allow the public in to see it without any authority knowing or caring what you are up to. Nor is there any obligation on the local police to see that you have your animals securely caged, which means that your collection of killers can be outside the law.

This frightens me very much indeed, as it does my father and the rest of the family, and it is something we have always tried to raise in television chat-shows and other programmes in which we have appeared. It is something the government will have to tackle. It is ridiculous that anyone can keep lions, hyenas or orang-utans without restraint, while it is necessary to buy a 37½p. licence for a chihuahua, or satisfy government inspectors before boarding a few domestic cats.

It is particularly disturbing that a monkey can be in a jungle in Borneo one day and in some English child's arms the next. The health risks are appalling; monkeys, for instance, can pass on a fatal brain disease (a form of encephalitis of which the virus is the most deadly known to man).

Nothing looks cuter than a cub sucking from a bottle, but how often do amateurs know what they are buying in the long term (or even, in some cases, in the short term)?

Do would-be pet-owners even realize in the first flush of buying that bush babies sleep all day and are active only at night? Do adults know that when a domesticated 'tea party' chimp gets to three years of age, it can bite a child's hand off; or that a badger cannot be kept safe except in a concrete shelter; or that an otter needs a stream to play in plus three pounds of whiting per day? A python, by the way (and these, too, are becoming popular as pets, for some kinky reason or other) will eat a *live* duck or a couple of live rabbits each fortnight when young, and a whole live calf a month when older. Alligators at nine inches are great to have and to show off, but what happens to them when they get three feet long; similarly, what becomes of fifteen-foot boa-constrictors that have started life at eighteen inches?

Also, it is certainly not difficult to gain the friendship of the apes but it is much more difficult to rid oneself of these faithful creatures after a time, and much heartbreak can follow.

Television must share the guilt for this boom in privately owned exotic animals. Advertising agents know that animals and children sell goods to the sentimental British better than anything. So lions, bears, tigers, crocs, elephants, chimps and even panthers are used in commercials which appeal to children. Whenever an animal gains success in this way, or otherwise hits the public heart (like Goldie the eagle's famous escape from London Zoo) thousands of children turn to their parents and say, '*That's* what we want for our birthdays.' And, the law being what it is, some of them get what they want without restraint.

Inevitably, many soon find they have bitten off more than they can chew; have taken on more than they can afford; or simply cannot get anybody to take their pets during the holidays. So they try to foist them on us, or on zoos, or they simply release their so-called pets surreptitiously, hoping for the best.

This is worst of all. The number of times we have been called out over the years because some poor frightened ex-pet was roaming the countryside is too distressing to recall. And I fear that it will get worse before it gets better. So I appeal to all readers of this book not to be moved sentiment-ally to raise wild animals because I do it all the time. I grew up with them. I am trained to it. It is a business with me as well as a pleasure. It's hard and dedicated work that simply cannot be undertaken part-time unless hurt and distress is to be wished on the animal or animals.

Having said all this, I must also point out another hazard people seldom consider in the enthusiasm of the moment. It is this. Although anybody can keep a wild animal, generally speaking, without restraint, there *are* responsibilities that go with such an action. In British law, it is the absolute duty of the owner of a wild animal to prevent it from escaping. If it does escape, the owner is liable for any injury or damage it may cause, which could be very serious indeed. And this still applies if the escape is due to the negligence of somebody else (as in leaving gates or doors open). Also, if an escaped wild animal manages to stay at liberty for years, its owner's liabil-ity for its actions still remains.

But if someone visits you to see your animals and is in-jured, or suffers damage, the law is not so simple.

In an amusing but to the point piece on 22 April, 1966, the *Solicitor's Journal* had this to say about 'Leo and the Law':

Whether March went out like a lamb or a lion, the stately homes season this year comes in like several lions—the lions at Longleat. The prudent traveller this year will not only, before setting out on his summer holiday, take out special insurance policies but also consult his solicitor about the risks he runs on safari amid England's ancestral glories. Lions we have no doubt are animals *ferae naturae*. Our visitors' host is therefore prima facie liable for whatever may happen. However, certain defences are open to him. If Little Johnny leans out of the car and tickles one of the beasts with a feather, an apportionment of liability under the Law Reform (Contributory Negligence) Act, 1945, may be expected in respect of such fur and other substances that might fly. But if, knowing the risks, you embark on this outing do you have a claim at all? Certainly the principle of *volenti non fit injuria* applies to dangerous animals: Behrens v. Bertram Mills Circus, Ltd. (1957) 2 Q.B.1. But does the latter-day Daniel in his family saloon really consent to all that may come? Knowledge of dangers does not constitute consent: Thomas v. Quartermaine (1887), 18 Q.B.D. 685, 696. The question is whether he really agreed to accept the risk. We suspect the answer must be that the visitor would not be there unless he believed that there was in fact no risk. Anyhow, there is one consolation for his lordship. A trespasser who enters without paying the fee has no action. Perhaps there would be a market at the gates for slot-machine life insurance like they have at airports?

Obviously as a professional I have to know the rules, and I take every instinctive or hard-learned precaution at The Pheasantry to prevent injuries to visitors. We even have a fire-bell, operated by the gate at the entrance to the garden, as an early warning to them, to us and to the animals.

But I refuse to over-restrain my brood, with the inevitable result that shins get nipped occasionally, or trousers torn and tights damaged. I would rather compensate a visitor than make life miserable for an animal.

And, despite what I have said above, I'm all for maximum contact, under reasonable control, between people and wild animals. They learn from each other . . . and I am very much of the opinion that we can learn much more from the animals than they can from us. There are so many ways in which they cope with life more successfully.

Take telepathy. It is much more highly developed in animals than in human beings. Lions can give each other precise orders and signals over vast distances.

Working with animals all the time, you acquire a strange depth of perception, recovering something that has long been numbed and overlaid by our civilization. Call it 'becoming more animal', if you like, but I for one am all for it. And in getting to know animals you get to know yourself better, which cannot be a bad thing.

We are certainly not the last word in life. Man is no more important or essential than an elephant or an ant, a sparrow or an eagle. Most of them were here before us. Some may be here long after we have destroyed ourselves.

I learn all too little about life from people, but I learn something new every day from my animals, and so can everyone.

I am tremendously proud of the pioneering we have done at Longleat and elsewhere. By breeding our semi-captive, well-cared-for animals, we expect to be able to re-stock wild acres in Africa with healthy and strong animals. And, in the process, I hope we can help to teach people how to go back to communing with the creatures of the wild instead of destroying them. In this important part in the balance of nature we may even learn again how to survive ourselves.

But, in passing, I do dearly wish that I could find the time to set up a school for the many British youngsters I hear from, who would love to look after wild animals—and would do it well with training—but who too often are frustrated in this ambition or go off half-cocked, in a do-it-yourself adventure with an animal in unhappy circumstances. My heart goes out to all would-be wild-animal lovers and trainers. But they must understand that this is one field in which sentimentality can be fatal and the advice has to be cruel to be kind.

I hope my book will give some second-hand pleasures to many such talented amateurs but, unless they are able somehow to acquire professionalism, I hope they will visit the well-run reserves now being created in most parts of the

country, and get fulfilment there, rather than add to the
unwanted-animal problem which almost daily (in pathetic
phone calls, letters and direct requests) causes me distress I
am seldom able to do something about, big though my heart
and 'orphanage' may be.

Chapter Fourteen

IN THE SWIM

On moonlit nights, Marquis, normally the soundest of sleep-
ers, would sometimes become restless and would pad silently
to the window, listening intently, his nostrils quivering to
catch the slightest scent which might bear a message from the
mysterious world beyond the garden. Those were almost the
only occasions when I would have misgivings about bringing
up African lion cubs in the protection of an English country
house.

I would slip out of bed, pick him up gently, feel the damp-
ness of his paws, which was at all times a giveaway to the
state of his mind, and would talk gently to him as we gazed
out into the wilds of moon-kissed Wiltshire. Was he sensing
the presence of so many of his own kind in the reserve, or
was he hearing other small creatures of the night near the
house—the nut-gnawings of bank voles, the faint shrilling of
shrews engaged in their endless bickerings, or even the
occasional squeak of the less-active dormouse? I could not
know. But I held him tight and warm against me and we
would look quietly for a time at the long tongues of moonlit
shadow licking the feet of the trees, as owls hooted across the
secret vastness of the parklands or a glow worm sought to
attract a mate to her lemon fire.

On such occasions, I would talk to Marquis in a voice of
sleepy love about any aspect of the world outside that occurred to me—about the lazy stars winking at us in the deep
sky; about the night odours of sweet musks and green acids;

or about the stately woods, spread out before us, tentacling into two counties.

Soon Marquis would be calm and we would creep back to bed, where his alarm clock awaited him and where Roger (too deep in sleep to notice our absence) had been keeping the nest *à trois* cosy and welcoming for us to return to sleep ready for a morning of increasing animal demands.

Because The Pheasantry had by now become a sort of conveyor-belt for reserve animals I had temporarily moved my ten-year-old Indian elephant, Donja, from the garage to nearby Stalls Farm. It was good of the farmer, Mr Charles Crossman, to take her, considering that she was seven feet tall and weighed over two tons. He had kindly offered a barn, so I boarded her out with him for a few months. A tortoiseshell cat already lived in the barn but they got along fine and soon became friends.

Elephants need exercise, so I would stroll over every day, with Marquis on his lead, and take Donja for a walk around Longleat park. The public, on the other hand, reacted in great surprise and delight at the sight, and the number of photographs taken of the three of us must run into many hundreds —unexpected leaves torn from a sunny day at Longleat.

A pets' corner was flourishing not far from the big house and we usually called in there when I had time. Marquis was marvellous with children and they all adored him. I have yet to see a child who is frightened of a lion cub. Donja could sometimes be sulky and on occasion would gallop off on her own over the fields, but on the whole she, too, got along well with people in her fashion.

The most embarrassing thing about taking Marquis and Donja out together was that the lion took to rolling in the elephant's droppings with obvious pleasure. Lions seem to be attracted to the smell.

The animals in more-or-less permanent residence at Pets' Corner included birds, rabbits, guinea pigs, a young bear, a baby chimp, a goat with three horns, a donkey, a wallaby and a tapir. Younger children often preferred to play with the pets rather than to be taken around the reserve with their parents, brothers and sisters, so we tried to see to it that they had as much fun as anyone. On quieter days I would convey several of my lion cubs there, perhaps together with Kumar, and a great time would be had by all, not least the lions, who can get bored with each other and relish human play-mates.

Just before Whit weekend, the excellent weather brought another rash of journalists and photographers intent this time on bearing good news to their summer-jaunting readers. Of course, we pulled out all the stops we could to give them individual stories. We had been used to their needs all our lives (as circuses depend on this co-operation just as much as lion parks) so we 'stood on our heads' if they requested it.

Richard, my elder brother, is marvellous with the press. Far too handsome for his own good, he looks what he is—a marvellous big game expert with a vast understanding of lions and other East African wild animals. But he is utterly fear-less, which can occasionally lead to complications.

Early one morning, Richard agreed to take an American magazine photographer with him in his open Land-Rover to get some special action pictures. It was a few hours before feeding time, so a couple of pieces of meat were placed at the back of the vehicle with the idea that Richard would drive through the park with lions leaping along behind, just unable to reach the tit-bits while the photographer banged away. Through the gate they went, with the photographer balanced behind Richard, his camera at the ready. The pictures would have been splendid if any had been taken. In the event, before they had gone far the photographer had dropped his camera and was hanging on for dear life.

The trouble was that Richard had misjudged the speed and staying power of some of Longleat's hungry young lions. Four of them had immediately taken up the chase. And they bounded after the Land-Rover with so much verve and gusto that Richard was forced to go at a speed that made picture-taking impossible. Indeed, at one stage, the lions were more or less breathing down the photographer's front collar stud!

Round the two-mile road they hurtled, with Richard shout-ing to the cameraman to jettison the beef and the poor fellow too petrified to do anything but hang on for dear life. Soon

Richard was rapidly running out of road, and, as he approached the exit gates, the lions seemed as strong as ever. A new problem arose because the gateman did not dare open up for the Land-Rover, so hard on its back wheels were the lions. Richard was therefore forced to swerve on to the grass by the gate, and was about to do a U-turn and do the two-mile circuit again in reverse; at this point Mike Lockyer, the warden, who was driving a tractor nearby, fortunately noticed what was happening and succeeded in heading the lions off until Richard could throw them the meat.

Afterwards, my brother was his usual phlegmatic self. To him it was all in the day's work. But the photographer had to have a large brandy and probably did not stop shaking until he got back to America.

Over Whit weekend, the public, with its unpredictability, remained our greatest worry . . . and will be, I am sure, in fifty years' time. They offer no constant pattern of behaviour. You never know what people will do next. We were better organized and better staffed than we had been at Easter, but the radio at The Pheasantry began to bleep out the most astonishing messages, together with the routine reports.

Almost unbelievable, but true, was the case of the lady in the chauffeur-driven limousine. She had no sooner entered the reserve than she got the chauffeur to take to the grass and drive her towards the nearest lion hut. She then got out of the car, climbed on the platform at the front of the hut and poked her head in the door, looking for lions.

The nearest patrol driver could see but scarcely credit all this as he hurtled towards her to avert a disaster. He was reasonably sure there were no lions in the hut, but he could not be 100 per cent certain. Leaping from his Land-Rover, he threw the fur-coated woman off the verandah and peered anxiously into the hut, his gun at the ready. It was empty. She was lucky. If she had disturbed and frightened a lioness with her cubs—or *any* lion, for that matter—it could have been her lot. The Lions of Longleat may look tame, but, like the visitors, they can be unpredictable.

Questioning revealed that the woman had never seen a lion before, not even in a cage. But she had read books about them and claimed she knew what she was doing, thanks to a deep well of intuition she said she possessed. A few sharp words from the game warden convinced her otherwise. Or I hope it did. As I say, you never know with people.

Breakdowns, too, seemed to happen when the patrols and breakdown waggon were just that tantalizing bit far from the scene. And it was incredible how quickly motorists forgot where they were in their anxiety to know what had gone wrong with their precious cars. They would jump out and get the bonnet up before anyone had realized they had broken down. Maybe they thought they could leap faster than a lion, if they had to get back in in a hurry. In this, they were certainly misguided.

There was the inevitable lady, too, who wound down all the windows of her car so that her five children could wave beach towels at the lions! Another was seen desperately emptying a bottle of orange squash into her boiling radiator.

And a trio of lions, for some unaccountable reason, took a liking to a Rolls-Royce (maybe because they could see their faces in it) and licked it all over with their rough tongues, to the horror of the occupants.

Some of the incidents were amusing in retrospect, although not very funny at the time. On Whit Monday, for instance, a car not only broke down in the reserve . . . it burst into flames as well. And its owner was faced with the shock choice of burning to death or being eaten by lions, or so he must have thought at that instant, as about a dozen beasts were gathering round him to see what it was about. But the patrols have fantastic reflex actions. And by the time the poor fellow had decided to face the lions, help was at his elbow.

But of all the idiotic actions, one which probably took the biscuit was that of a disabled driver who was found by an amazed patrolman to be sitting with his legs dangling out of his three-wheeled-car, within a short distance of a group of approaching lions. He explained blithely that his doctor had told him to do this every few miles to ease his circulation problems. He nearly cured them permanently!

Whether for publicity or through foolhardiness, a well-educated young man also gave us a fright by ignoring the now numerous warning signs in the reserve. Driving round with his wife, he suddenly hopped out of his car to face what he later called 'a really sweet little lion'. Before he knew it, he was surrounded by lions and only the vigilance of the wardens saved him. 'You don't understand,' he was protesting volubly. 'They like me. I have a special relationship with lions.' He was escorted from the park.

Later that evening there was another anxiety. Weakened presumably by the severe frosts of the winter and spring, a 160-foot elm tree crashed on top of one of the timber lion huts. Fortunately they were strongly built ex-banana wagons, so it did no great damage except for scaring a pride and starting a bit of a lion-stampede around the stockade. Fortunately, too, it happened after all the visitors had gone for the day. Great care had been taken before we opened to check every suspect tree in the reserve for weakness (and branches had been lopped from trees in the vicinity of the fence to prevent any tree-climbing lions leaping to freedom) but somehow nature managed to spring this surprise and there, as a challenge, was this enormous tree overhanging the hut.

At once four woodmen, under head forester, Derek Riley, were called in and while an ex-Kenyan hunter stood guard, with a 500-calibre rifle, they set to work lopping the branches and cutting up the trunk. The lions were very curious to know what was going on and gathered round in a circle, but the woodmen were laconic about it. 'It makes a change from a few squirrels and the odd badger,' said Mr Riley. By morning all the debris had been dragged away and the public were unaware that yet another 'incident' had occurred in our lion experiment.

No sooner were the headaches of the holiday weekend over than another was added when Joe, the South American tapir, burrowed out of Pets' Corner and disappeared. We hunted everywhere for him for days but he was nowhere to be seen. Apart from being valuable (at about £350) and rather rare, Joe was a great favourite. Fully grown at two years, and dark brown, he is rather like a pig which has acquired an elephant trunk; a hoofed mammal, he is, in fact, a distant relative of the rhinoceros.

We were all rather sad about Joe, doubting whether he could survive in the wild. Then, one morning at breakfast, as I was walking Donja and Marquis on the grass between the lake and the drive leading to Longleat House, both of them reacted so violently to something in the bushes that, before I knew anything was amiss, the elephant had reared up on his hind legs and Marquis had had to leap for his young life. In the upset I let go of Marquis's lead and, before I could recover it, he was off into the rhododendrons near the lake in pursuit of something invisible to me. I followed at speed (Donja having taken off into the blue, to be rounded up later) and I soon saw Joe, the tapir, hoofing it for the water with Marquis only inches away.

Longleat gets its name from the 'long stream', the River Leat, which runs through the grounds in front of the house. Lancelot Capability Brown created the very beautiful Half-Mile Pond (as the lake is called) in the eighteenth century by damming the river and making an island in the centre, but it is unlikely that he could have foreseen for it anything remotely resembling the performance which now followed.

Joe plunged into the lake, leaving Marquis panting on the bank. Scarcely considering what I was doing, I dived after the surely swimming tapir. As I surfaced, I heard an agonized whine from Marquis and then a splash. The brave little lion was in the water behind me, paddling away for dear life.

An instant dilemma was created, I can tell you, what with Joe making good progress towards renewed freedom and my favourite lion manfully swimming after me. I did not want the tapir to escape. Nor did I want Marquis to get into difficulties. All I could think of doing, in the moment of crisis and excitement, was to recall and make use of a long-forgotten life-saving drill. I back-pedalled for a moment, gathered Marquis to me, placed his front paws round my neck, his big head close to mine, and carried on swimming as he held tight and yelped a little, his buoyant body jerking along underneath me like a furry 'Mae West'.

It was only about fifty yards to the island, which was where Joe was heading fast. We made it just a few yards behind the tapir and scrambled out. Marquis paused only to shake himself vigorously, dog-fashion, before following me into the brambles in pursuit of Joe. It was a mad scamper and, of course, being a wily little tapir, he shot clean through and out the other side into the water again, while I was struggling with the prickly bushes. So when we in turn reached the water, there was nothing for it but for me to take Marquis round my neck again and swim in. By this time the lion was enjoying it as much as if it was a game in The Pheasantry, and I was beginning to see the funny side, too. Marquis had loosened his grip on my throat a little, so I was able to do a sort of fast doggy-paddle crawl across the second fifty-yard stretch, instead of the breast stroke I had used before, and I actually touched the tapir a few yards out from the far bank, but was unable to grasp his slippery body as he scrambled ashore.

Off Joe went, across the half-mile of grass towards Prospect Hill, with one very tired girl and one very wet lion in hot pursuit. Just before he reached the bushy heights where I could almost certainly have lost him I pounced and landed on top of the tapir, upon which he bit me on my largely bare chest for my pains. And as I let go, he would have got away had not Father, Richard and Mike Lockyer arrived at that moment, alerted by the night-watchman, Anthony Horler, and clued up as to our exact location by our combined grunts and squawks.

In a moment it was over. Mike put a wrestler's leg lock on Joe's head and Richard quickly hog-tied his back legs.

Then they sat back roaring with laughter, and looking down I could almost see the joke. There I was, jeans and shirt dripping, my long hair hanging round my shoulders in damp rats' tails, and goose pimples rapidly taking over my body, the water having been colder than cold. And there was a sheepish little lion nuzzling his damp head into me, not knowing quite what was going on any more.

Before accepting Richard's jacket, I tickled Marquis behind the ears, kissed his nose and told him what a brave lion he was swimming after me, never having been in the water before. I was really proud of him.

Chapter Fifteen

... AMONG THE DANDELIONS

Joe, the errant tapir, really started something when he led Marquis into the lake. Thereafter the little lion was water crazy and infected the other cubs with his enthusiasm. Almost every day when out for exercise, they would swim in the small pond where they had so recently skated. I had had occasion in the past, in Africa and India, to swim with a panther, a leopard and a couple of lions in stunts for films, so I was not surprised that young lions should enjoy the water. What did surprise me was that they liked cold English water, because that is what it was at The Pheasantry, even in late May.

Kumar, too, enjoyed a swim. Now nearly six months old and weighing nearly as much as I did, he frightened visitors rather when they came upon him frolicking in the woods by the pond.

Tigers are becoming extremely rare on the face of the earth (and, indeed, at the present rate of decline it has been estimated that they will be extinct in thirty years). In the wild they have only managed to escape complete wiping-out as people take over their territories by adapting to all kinds of unattractive terrain. Some, in fact, have had to become semi-aquatic by living among the islands of the Indian deltas. It was my hope to find a suitable mate for Kumar and breed some healthy young tigers as well as lions at Longleat.

Tigers are affectionate, if they take to you at all, but never demonstrative in the way of lions. When he came out of the water after a swim, Kumar would give me one lick with his rough tongue and would then settle down with a bone he had invariably brought with him, dog-fashion, on our outings.

Not so Marquis. His swim over, he would monopolize me for attention and affection. I was now very pregnant and not too energetic, so rather than play games, I would talk to Marquis about the other wild creatures around.

May was ending in glorious sunshine and Longleat was teeming with life. The rhododendrons and azaleas, among the loveliest to be found in England, were at their best, and the tall trees were rostrums for birds, all with different songs to sing, all with their individual plumages.

The English birds were totally unafraid of the lions and tiger and would come within inches of large paws and jaws without a hint of unnaturalness or unfamiliarity on either side. As each new bird appeared, I would explain its characteristics to Marquis and he would cock his sweetly rounded ears as if he was a bright pupil at a nature lesson. There was plenty to talk about. The late spring had led to almost a traffic jam of arriving birds, all eager to signify their presence . . . the cuckoo's wandering voice; the streamlined silhouette of the swallow; the first swifts and turtle-doves; chiffchaff, willow-warbler and black cap in their various niches; green-finches singing like billy-o, fluttering in small circles and beating their wings so slowly as to remain in the air but only just . . . ; whitethroats, un-English, dancing up and down; black cawing rooks and hysterically shrieking jays; sedge and reed warblers by the edge of the pond; the yellow-hammer, too, with his fireman's helmet head and his scared expression —what a wealth of bird life there is in Wiltshire in the early summer.

'Pink-pink!' went a chaffinch in the lower branches of the elm under which I was sitting.

'Look, Marquis,' I would say, 'you can tell the chaffinch by his white corporal's stripes on his black wings. Hasn't he a fine blue head and such a pretty rosy breast, and see how he puffs it out to make him look bigger, just as you do sometimes. His wife's a corporal, too, but her coat is a much more drab dull green.

'And that's a greedy blackbird over there with the yellow

beak, stealing the grubs from the sparrows. But see the hedge-sparrow that's just arrived, with his scissor-bill flashing. He's greedy, too. There'll be a fight in a minute . . .'

So I would go on. It was strange this habit I had acquired of talking to Marquis, as if he were a child. But I would not have done it had I not believed that he understood and wanted to know more.

One day, Marquis astonished me by emerging from the brown waters of the pond with a fish in his mouth. He brought it to me at once and dropped it in my lap, wrinkling his nose the while in apparent disgust. It appeared to be a carp, which surprised me, too, for they are bottom-living fish and I had not seen Marquis diving deep. As it appeared to be uninjured, I threw it back in the pond, scolding and restraining Marquis and the others—they having gathered around, interested in the wriggling creature their friend had captured. I had not thought of lions as retrievers up to that point, but later I was to discover that anything a game dog can do a young lion can do with as much natural zest. The pond provided many adventures for the cubs. The 'kur-r-rucking' of water hens at full throttle would raise a vole, or perhaps the vole had caused their flight, and off the pack would go in crazy pursuit. Croaking frogs would be nosed out of the reeds, or shrews. Occasionally a kingfisher would visit us, but he would be left in peace to seek his prey.

Crossing the fields, some with their lush grass sprinkled with buttercups, daisies, dandelions and patches of sorrel, and others lying fallow, canaried with flowering mustard, we would start up a family of rabbits and there would be a great scurrying and flashing of white tails, followed by pokered tufted tails, before they would escape the lions by disappearing into a burrow. Hares, with no burrows in which to hide, would have to rely on their great speed to get away, bounding over the grass in leaps of ten feet and more.

It was after such a chase that Marquis met a safari of snail hunters. My sister, Margaret, had been out with us. It had begun to rain and she had rounded up Kumar and the other four lion cubs, while I chose to wander back more slowly with Marquis, as I idly chewed a piece of grass and drank in the sunshine as an antidote to the weight of my child. Suddenly, when we rounded a bend in the normally deserted lane, there they were, a gathering of villagers, poking and prodding along the hedgerow, seeking out their mute, defenceless tiger-striped quarry among the beds of nettles. In an instant, Marquis was amongst them and they were scattering like leaves in a gale, throwing away their sticks in panic.

As I grabbed Marquis by the collar, I called out my reassurances to the fearful hunters and they gradually gathered round to gaze in wonder at 'the lady and the lion'. With Marquis inquisitively sniffing by my side, I got the villagers to show me which were the edible snails. They had an astonishing gift for finding these mouth-watering molluscs, always a popular delicacy in the south-west. Where I could see no trace, they would flatten some vegetation, move some stones, and reveal gregarious colonies, newly awake from hibernation. They offered me some to eat, but snails are not to my taste, so I declined politely and dragged the unwilling, intrigued Marquis away, leaving the hunters to get on with their commercial enterprise.

This and a hundred other ways did my little lion learn English ways among the dandelions and native creatures around Longleat.

Chapter Sixteen

MARQUIS, THE GUARD LION

Next to swimming, Marquis's greatest joy in life was to be taken for a ride in my car—a BMC 1100 in those days. He would sit up in the passenger seat squeaking and grunting his reactions to everything that happened as we bowled along. The responses of other drivers and pedestrians, especially when we stopped at traffic lights, were hilarious to see. But (as I had occasion to point out to the occasional police car which stopped me in wonderment after chases inspired by reports from bemused motorists), there is nothing in English law which says I cannot drive around with a *live* noddy-headed lion as a companion, in the front, instead of one of those ridiculous stuffed, mechanical ones other drivers have on the back shelf.

I took Marquis to galas and fêtes all around Wiltshire and he officially opened a store when he was three months old. Everywhere he drew the crowds and everywhere, after the first astonished reactions, he was lionized and petted. As Marquis came more and more in demand—sometimes being booked for two fêtes in one day—I was forced to cheat a little and send Major in his place occasionally. Although Major was taller, had a squint and looked different altogether (with a paler-coloured mane and no under-belly mane—only tufts on his elbows) this was never detected.

Occasionally, where overnight stays were necessary I would have to sneak Marquis into my hotel room wherever we happened to be. I never declared him, sure that no manager, however liberal-minded, would allow a fairly large lion to share a room with its mistress. I had trained him to keep absolutely still when ordered to do so, in order that I could sneak him in under a coat—no easy task, considering his weight and my condition!

It became quite a pantomime, sometimes repeated several times a week. I would sign in first and get the room key (having left Marquis in the car in the nearest side street) explaining that my luggage would be arriving later. I would then sneak out, get hold of Marquis and totter in drunkenly but quickly, staggering upstairs rather than using the lift with the limp bundle hidden by my fur coat or a rug. I would then lock Marquis in the bathroom (always having booked a room with bathroom) and would at last bring the car round to the hotel to disgorge my luggage proper. When it had been taken up, I would invariably collapse exhausted in a chair, useless for an hour or so.

Inevitably, in the mornings there would be alarming near-misses, as when chambermaids wanted to clear up and were stopped more or less with their hands on the door of the 'lion's den'. But, fortunately, my ploys were never discovered.

David and two friends

The equestrian lion: Marquis and Jarro, Mary's Spanish Lippizaner stallion

Marquis, the enthusiastic motorist

Tea-break: Marquis helps the builders of the new restaurant at Longleat, March 1968

Introductions: David meets Wamba, our five-year-old African elephant

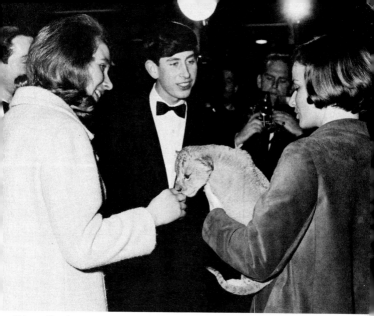

Prince Charles and Princess Anne meet one of Mary's lion cubs at the Olympia Circus

All good friends

Mary with Phoenix, the two-year-old black panther

Mr. Jim's first steps, one hour old, in the Reserve at Longleat

David, Charles and the four D's: Dougal, Doshi, Daniel and Dago

Mary rides Arnold on his arrival at Longleat in 1967

Indeed, I do the same sort of thing with other cubs to this day.

I was now resuming my film and television work, which had been interrupted by the exigencies of the Longleat reserve, and, having been signed up to perform miracles in the forthcoming film, *Dr Dolittle*, I had been rounding up domestic cats to train, to supplement one of my own, Tomasina (who had starred in the Disney film of that name). At least thirty cats were required for an important sequence in the picture. Wild cats I had in plenty, but these had to be domestic ones and there seemed no easy way of rounding up so many at short notice for training. Scrawny stray moggies from cats' homes just would not do. These had to be healthy and tractable specimens. I knew they would be well-fed and cared for on location, and I was perfectly prepared to find them good homes after the film.

The American company making the film brought over three animal trainers from the States to the pretty Wiltshire village of Castle Combe which was to be the main English location. They also brought a dog (which was never used) two chimps, and two sea-lions. One of the seals was sick and would not eat, so I had to keep him in a bath at The Pheasantry for two weeks. He arrived to English rain from Florida sun and took badly to the change. He would just lie there moaning sadly. He stank of fish and of illness. But we pulled him round and cheered him up. Soon he was great company again. He would pick things up at request, he loved 'clapping his hands' and, most of all, he relished blowing kisses to all and sundry.

I also had to organize two cows to take part in the film and had to train them to shake a leg on request. I bought two Jerseys from a local dairy herd and kept them in the orchard of The Pheasantry (which is part of the back garden) while I trained them. I also milked them every day, which was quite a problem of belly-to-belly manoeuvring, so large was I with child by that time!

A Hereford bull was also supposed to be involved in the proceedings, but he was written out of the script at a fairly early stage.

D

My father had been made technical adviser in England for all animals in *Dr Dolittle* and among his special contributions was to hire and train some hounds from the Duke of Beaufort's pack. And, meanwhile, I was schooling five foxes (raised from cubs and perfectly tame) to run loose to order. Their part was to be one in which they trotted out of a house, across a yard and through a trapdoor into a barn.

My grey horse, Jarro, had a fairly important part in *Dolittle* and five of my other horses had 'walk-on and lie down' roles.

These were fairly routine disciplines. Nor was it a problem training a skunk which was to be featured. He did not have much to do and the main trick was in persuading him not to bite anyone. But before he could be transported to the location, it was necessary to have his smell taken away. This is done by cutting out the appropriate glands. The local vet, who had tackled many problems for us over the years, had never had to de-scent a skunk before. But he did the job immaculately.

A circus was also required for a spectacular sequence in the film. My father went around every circus in England until he found one that fulfilled the requirements for *Dr Dolittle*. The one he chose was Roberts Bros, quite a big, four-pole affair, with elephants, horses, lions, tigers, chimps and bears. He had to persuade the Roberts Bros to take three summer weeks off at the height of their tour, and he had to see that the film company reimbursed them handsomely for this. Of course, in the end the weather was so bad and the delays so substantial that the circus had to stand about for three weeks doing nothing and the circus sequence in the film had to be re-created later in America.

Anyway, early in June, I shipped my various animals to Castle Combe to get them acclimatized and familiarized before shooting would begin later in the month. And, although he was not hired for the film, I took Marquis along in my caravan. He was by now so much a part of my life that we would have pined for each other. I could talk to Roger, my husband, on the telephone, but Marquis would have to share my bed and my adventures.

Castle Combe is the picture-postcard village which was voted the loveliest in England in 1962. The film company, Twentieth Century Fox, in the course of spending the largest original budget it had ever authorized, had set about temporarily rebuilding parts of the village to create the illusion that it was the fictional early-Victorian fishing port of Puddleby-on-the-Marsh.

Some of the villagers resented the intrusion on their privacy and a hard-core minority fought furiously and bitterly, even after we had all assembled there, to prevent the little town's use in the picture. A couple of dissidents went so far as to resort to violence. In a much-publicized incident (which did not do the film any harm in terms of press coverage) they were only just thwarted in an attempt to blow up a sandbag dam. This had been built in the stream that runs through the centre of Castle Combe to create a harbour. There were some other and lesser incidents but in the main the villagers were well rewarded for any inconvenience. Every spare room in the place was rented, restaurants boomed, villagers became extras, tourists arrived in their thousands and shops did tremendous trade.

Over the years, my animals, wild and tame, have appeared in every film Walt Disney has made in this country, about a dozen in all (and he gave me a medal before he died in appreciation of my services) and in many others here and abroad. These have included *Casino Royale, Chitty-Chitty-Bang-Bang, David Copperfield, Oliver Cromwell, The Southern Star, Maya, Crooks and Coronets, Masquerade, Jane Eyre, One Million Years BC, The Long Duel, 2001* and *Julius Caesar*.

Dr Dolittle was unusual for me, in that it did not involve any of my wild animals. The sequences with lions and other big game were being filmed in the West Indies and in Hollywood. Indeed, my work in the film was a bit of a pushover compared to some I had been involved in. The longest 'act' I had to put on was the parade of my thirty cats in pursuit of Anthony Newley (playing Dolittle's Irish catmeat-man friend Matthew Mugg) along the village street. To this end, a long run was prepared to my directions (like a meshed-in street) and I soon had the cats trained that they were only fed if they did the simple trick of trotting in procession along the 'street'. It was as easy as that. The only slight snag was that one or two of the thirty escaped from time to time and sometimes, assisted by zealously willing children I would round up the wrong cats in the village. It became quite amusing when villagers found they had the wrong cat and had to come to my 'cattery' to claim their own. They took it very well. I was forever counting the tabbies, too, because sometimes, after a round-up, I would find myself with more than thirty and the 'unofficial stray' would have to be weeded out from the others. Although I know all my lions and other 'wild cats' by looks and personality, I never quite got to know all the domestic cats at Castle Combe by name or appearance, hence the constant mix-ups.

The atmosphere among the film community in the village was terrific, but as always in film-making, the worst aspect was having to hang around for weeks to take part in a few hours of filming. Also, the weather was so mixed that some sequences were delayed or cancelled. I was very glad of Marquis's company. He slept with me in the caravan at nights (all fifty pounds of him) and he also played his part in the activities of the film company—as a guard lion!

There was quite a community of caravans and other vehicles, loaded with valuable props, equipment and stars, around the field. So I strung a long wire between stakes and linked Marquis's chain to it so that he could move freely for quite a distance. At four months, he looked frighteningly large and ferocious, although he was still a baby in every way, if you knew him; and he did a better job for the film company than a dozen Securicor men could have done.

The chain had now become a necessity, in leading him about as well as in tethering him, because he had chewed through two leather leads and a rope in the previous week or two. He had also taken to chewing the end of his tail in bed, or, if he could not reach it, because my unborn child and I were taking up too much space, he would chew holes in the blankets!

Early every morning, before people were about, Marquis

would have a swim in the village stream and I would go in with him whenever I could. Appropriately, in the context of the all-animal film, Marquis was able to follow exciting scents and make the further acquaintance of English native creatures. In the course of our leisurely outings around the well-populated hedge and stream banks, he would stalk or play hide-and-seek with such inhabitants as stealthy stoat, rapacious rat, wily weasel . . . and heroic hedgehog. I was floating happily on my back in the stream before breakfast one day when there was the most frightful flurry of spitting and scratching from the bank. I splashed over just in time to stop Marquis doing himself an injury as he poked with his paw at a ball of protective prickles at the hedge bottom, head and tail tucked well in, spikes bristling in all directions. I dragged the reluctant lion back into the water and allowed the brave little hedgehog (ever willing to fight when cornered) to make his burrowing escape into the thick leaves.

The shallows in the stream were teeming with miniature life—a marvellous place, no doubt, when the film crew were not there, for small boys to collect frog spawn, tiddlers and tadpoles. Dragonflies intrigued and sometimes annoyed my swimming lion, as they flitted fairy-like around his head— graceful slendernesses of colour, red, blue, yellow and black, appearing only when the sun shone and going off to impersonate pieces of twig among the leaves when it rained . . . as it did almost every day we were at Castle Combe. Flaming June was a very damp squib that year.

Dragonflies I can bear, even when they brush my face, but I am petrified of insects in general. Indeed, on my very first safari in Africa, I disgraced myself by screaming when I went to bed in my tent the first night, because I thought some monster insect was about to attack me. When Richard and some armed native bearers dashed in, expecting to find me facing a lion at the very least, I was cowering in a corner trying to get away from—of all things— a grasshopper! The lamplight had magnified it and my imagination had done the rest.

Castle Combe seemed to be a paradise for insects, so it was hell for me. Apart from extra-large wasps, bees and hornets,

I was forever dodging beetles and bugs, daddy-longlegs, cock-chafers and centipedes. Ugh! And I had to restrain Marquis from digging up or pawing the many long, slimy worms, multiplied by the rain, which were eating the brown soil and making their casts near the stream. Grasshoppers, too, came from nowhere after the showers and leapt around us like monkeys, happy among the sharp odours of roots and nettles.

Occasionally, we would stumble on the body of a bird or some other small dead creature and I would have to warn Marquis away from the crowded, silent-roaring city the carcass had usually become, inhabited by flies, ants and grubs. I did not want any of them to get into his coat to his discomfort. It is a strange, eerie experience to stumble thus, in the midst of a summer day, on death the destroyer, whose work goes on all the time, although we so seldom catch him at it.

In all ways, the vast, brimming world of nature seemed fuller and more concentrated around this beautiful agrarian microcosmic Wiltshire village than anywhere I had ever been, but perhaps it was because I was stuck there with time on my hands, and too little to do, for six long weeks of midsummer. Marquis slept a lot, when visitors and crew permitted, and of an afternoon we would lie together under the trees near the caravan, amid patches of sorrel and wide ringlets of darker grass under which potent spawn was lurking sleepily until September, when it would erupt overnight to thrust up giant mushrooms for the picking. Around us were purple orchids, wild strawberry flowers, foxgloves, wild honeysuckle and cuckoo spit—the last-named not a flower but the beady froth created by an insect, the frog-hopper, who had sucked the sap from plants and churned it into foam by using his hind legs as a beater.

Hares were Marquis's greatest preoccupation at Castle Combe. There were lots of them around and it was his obvious ambition and intention to catch one. With no burrows in which to hide, they would squat in their rough nests or 'forms' in the grass and would be off like the wind as soon as they picked up our scent. But when we happened to approach with the wind in our faces we got quite close to them once or twice and one or two nearly met their ends in a swipe from a lion's paw. This game went on almost daily throughout our stay and it was only bad luck that prevented Marquis making his first kill.

Owls were also numerous around the village but the few times we were out together after dark Marquis made it clear that he liked them as little as I did—especially the ghost-like barn owl, with its white shape and screeching voice . . . but no doubt these and the brown owls were appreciated by the farmers, living, as they do, on the larvae and pupae of insects —leather-jackets, wireworm, cockchafers and so on. We even had a nightingale to entertain us as we lay together in those wordless nights in the secret stillness of the caravan.

It was strange to have become a caravan-dweller again. The Pheasantry was my first permanent home after a lifetime in the circus, broken mainly by unhappy spells at boarding and finishing schools. Even when I ran one of the first deep-littered beef farms in England (with 400 head of cattle) at Stockbridge, Hants, between leaving the circus and opening up the reserve at Longleat I lived in a caravan rather than in the farmhouse.

Indeed, I was born in a circus caravan. It was touch and go that I did not emulate Judy Garland by being cradled in a trunk in a dressing room at the London Palladium. I had chosen to arrive in the 'close season' for circuses, on 26th November, 1937, to be exact. The family circus was in winter quarters in Hampshire and my father was keeping his hand in by appearing twice-nightly on the stage of the famous theatre wrestling with a big brown Caucasian bear, named Bruni. He was well down the bill which was not inappropriately headed by the Crazy Gang. More by luck than by judgment I suppose, my mother, Rosie Purchase (a skilled lion-trainer from another famous circus family, by the way) did not happen to be at the Palladium tethering the bear the night I was born. So I arrived in the back-yard of a Kentish Town pub where our caravan had rested for the winter, surrounded by various lion, tiger and bear cubs—my very first companions and playmates. It *would* be somewhere romantic like that!

Now here I was in a caravan again, with only a lion for

company and lots of time to think about the direction in which my life was taking me. Until the almost unbelievable success of Father's Longleat adventure, I had been something of a strayer and a loner. In the same way that birds can be divided up into resident and migratory types, so can people. There are strayers and stayers. Without stayers, there would be no planners, no governments, no banks and no civil servants. Without strayers, I am pleased to think, there would be fewer new ideas or adventures.

I never got into a rut, as the stayers do. I always had to be on the move and doing things. When I was at school, I spent much of the time looking out of the windows, envying the birds their freedom. The sky always seemed huge with adventure I was missing. The poppies dancing in the field were so much more wonderful than the boring ballet lessons in the gym.

Strayers are gamblers and Longleat was one of the great gambles of all time, so I took to it with all the enthusiasm of the strayer-born. So did Roger, my husband. He is even crazier in this respect than I am. Born into a banking family, he suddenly threw up a safe and successful career in a bank to join a circus and went on to become general manager, for eight years, of one of the greatest shows on earth . . . until I married him and led him into other adventures (including camel-dealing in the market places of the Middle East during our honeymoon!).

Strayers both, we had settled at The Pheasantry because no two days were alike and we were able to keep and train our own animals there as well as being involved in the reserve. Straying is a secret, ever changing process in which new pockets of discovery and challenge are forever being thrown up and enjoyed. We lived in a house at Longleat, but we have caravans in the yard and we are always ready and eager to sally forth in search of life's few remaining Gardens of Eden.

Chapter Seventeen

THE SAGA OF THE HAIRY PAW

Each night I would telephone Roger from Castle Combe and each night he would give me news of the cubs, the pets, the horses and the lions in the park.

The love life of the lions was of particular concern as summer followed spring. The fairly intensive sex life within the prides had resulted in a number of pregnancies and several births had been notified by wardens.

The first cub conceived at Longleat—there having been others conceived in quarantine—was born to a lioness named Plymouth, at the roadside on 12 June, just nine weeks after the opening of the reserve. The first anyone knew of the great event was when a visitor drove across to a patrol driver with the news that he had just witnessed and photographed the arrival of a young lion on a grass bank near the entrance. Within the hour, Plymouth had shown herself to be disinterested in her cub. Indeed, she had wandered off with her pride and Roger had had to scoop up the cub from the roadside and take it home to bottle-feed.

This incident apart, the wardens, as instructed, kept away from the confinements, leaving the mothers safe in the cool shade and straw of their log cabins for the first few days. But soon it was confirmed to me that Mary (one of my favourites, of course) had produced three excellent cubs and that four more had been born to a big six-year-old lioness, Sheba. Mary's three were suckled and loved, but two of Sheba's four disappeared, presumably eaten, soon after birth and she was then seen walking off with the other two in her mouth to a corner of the reserve; so, to prevent further disasters, they were taken away from her and were now in The Pheasantry also.

One of these cubs was named Mr Merritt, after the Warminster rural surveyor of that name who had been more than helpful to us in our planning applications. He was thrilled at the honour. And the other (at the suggestion of the local Young Conservatives, whose emblem is a lion) was called Winston.

There were still occasional fights in the reserve, Roger told me, due mainly to sexual jealousies, territorial demands, or the fact that a lion developed an illness or infirmity and was regarded as a weakling.

Atlas, who had been severely injured on press day by three other lions, was now back in the reserve, fully recovered and successfully re-established. But Rema, an elderly lioness, had developed a limp and was so badly mauled one day before anyone could get to her that Richard had had to get her out and take her to our Southampton zoo to live in peace. And one other sad day, a lion named Caesar had developed some illness, unknown to anyone, and was all but killed by the pride before help could get there. It was necessary, alas, for the vet to put Caesar down. This was our only fatality that first season, but it was saddening news nonetheless.

Celebrities galore were now visiting the reserve, Roger reported, including Miss Israel, Egon Ronay (who apparently sniffed rather contemptuously at the food that was being given to the lions) and Billy Walker. The last-named was accompanied by his brother, George, who was heard instructing the boxer, 'If one of them lion geezers attacks, open with a right-cross, see, and then fell 'im wif yer left-uppercut!'

A team of Russian delegates had also visited the park and the leader, Deputy Director of Light Industry, Mr Levenkov, immediately pounced on one of our four-and-elevenpenny souvenir metal Longeat lions, and said, 'I recognize these.' He was right. They are stamped 'Made in USSR.' Theirs had been the cheapest tender, and we always try to give good value for money.

I was missing the excitement, and I was being missed by the 'orphanage' animals, too, according to Roger, so it was a great pleasure to be able to get away from Castle Combe for a day when Marquis was called on to do duty as a living, breathing, all-action version of World Cup Willie, the soccer mascot. The occasion was the arrival at Longleat of sixteen of the World Cup soccer referees (including Swiss Gottfried Dienst, who was to referee the England-Germany final, a charming man who insisted on recounting all the English swear words he had been swotting up for the occasion!).

Marquis squatted nobly on the steps of Longleat House for the photographers, a Union Jack draped round him and the Marquess of Bath by his side. There followed the inevitable dark hints that if Herr Dienst did not let England win, he would be thrown to the lions, and a marvellous day was had by all.

Back in my caravan with Marquis, I happened to be listening to the radio a day or two later when a news announcer said something about an aeroplane pilot battling with three ferocious lions. I pricked up my ears and Marquis obligingly did likewise. 'A Swiss Globe twin-engined Dart Herald made an emergency landing at Brussels today,' the voice was going on (and I was now taking in every word), 'on its way from Frankfurt to London. When it was at 5,000 feet above Belgium, three dangerous lions it was carrying broke out of their crates and threatened to maul and possibly eat the crew. On descending rapidly and landing at Brussels Airport, the pilot and navigator broke open the cockpit windows and leapt out. A net was then thrown over the nose of the plane and police with sub-machine-guns cordoned off the area until help could be summoned from a zoo.'

I was absolutely flabbergasted. Indeed, as Frankie Howerd would say, my flabber was utterly gasted. These were three lion *cubs* bound for quarantine at Plymouth Zoo before being released at Longleat. They were part of a consignment of thirteen from Abyssinia, all of them hand-reared around the Imperial Palace. Lord and Lady Bath had selected them on a trip to Addis Ababa, during which they had been royally received by the Emperor, the legendary Lion of Judah (whose private collections of lions was second only to ours in size). The Emperor was particularly appreciative of their visit because he had spent some time at Longleat during his wartime exile. These marvellous black-maned lions we had secured in this way, and which we hoped would eventually still further improve our breeding stock, were all babies.

I had been notified that the first three were on their way by air via Frankfurt and I know that one of them (Little Sheba) was eight weeks old, while the other two (Percy and Olaf) were about twelve weeks. I was therefore absolutely staggered to hear these 'pets' described as 'ferocious lions'. I got on the telephone within minutes, and found that Roger had already been on to Brussels, where a lady zoo-director soon had everything sorted out, explaining to everyone who would listen that they were harmless cubs.

Re-crated, the little lions reached London Airport early the next day in the same plane but with another crew, and I was there to meet them, anxious to be sure they had come to no harm at the hands of the original aircrew, one of whom was reported to have held them at bay with an axe. They were fine, and were soon on their way by road to Plymouth.

Of course, the morning papers blew the story up beautifully into a King-Kong-like drama, with quotes like—

'PILOT: "I suddenly saw a hairy paw against my leg . . ."'

But the most delightful excerpt, picked up by all the reporters was this:

'PILOT TO CONTROL TOWER: "I've got lions in my cockpit."
'CONTROL TOWER TO PILOT: "Stick them in your tank!"'

It was an incredible non-event while it lasted.

Meanwhile, two more fine lions were successfully transported from Dublin, as deck cargo on the Bristol Steam Navigation Company's good ship *Hero*, without the captain diving into the drink!

At Castle Combe, I had settled down again, drilling my cats and enjoying life with Marquis. The film crew had really taken to the lion and vice versa, and one day they got together a picnic for him on a low table, beautifully laid, outside the caravan. The centrepiece was a couple of superb joints of beef from the local butcher, done up with ribbon with Marquis's name on, like a beauty queen' s sash.

I had kept Marquis in the caravan until all was ready, but as soon as he saw the feast he was at it. He pounced on the table,- sweeping the decorations clear with his tail and dragging the meat away to his accustomed corner, while the delighted crew snapped away with their cameras. It was an undignified scene, but there was no doubt that the offerings were appreciated, as Marquis's belchings underlined.

Later, as we were all having tea around the steps, Marquis, who had finished his splendid feast (and who would normally have settled down for a snooze) suddenly decided to be less than grateful for the treat. Before I could restrain him, he had grabbed an unguarded camera and was shaking it in his teeth to the point that I had to tap him on the nose to make him release it. Miraculously, no serious damage was done and the owner was good enough to laugh about it. This was so out of character that I felt it was high time he was back in the family discipline of his 'home'.

Marquis was a bit dubious, too, about the domestic cats I had assembled for the film, perhaps because I was having to pay them a lot of attention. I tried to make him more gracious towards them—a mistake as it was to turn out—but to no avail.

Eventually, the cameras turned for the last time on Anthony Newley, his barrel of fish and the thirty pursuing cats, and (my other animals having already done their stuff) I was able to roll back to Longleat and goodness only knew what problems.

Chapter Eighteen

SAD DAYS AT THE PHEASANTRY

It was now the beginning of August, with my baby due in six or seven weeks, and the reserve was doing ever more fantastic business. Characteristically, from the moment he had sniffed the first whiff of success, Father had been eyeing the spare acres of deer park around and beyond the perimeter fences of the lion reserve. He was also often to be found brooding on the banks of Half-Mile Pond. He was not saying much, and he is not the sort of man you ever question closely, but a clue was to be found in the fact that he and Richard had been trapping and shipping far more exotic miscellaneous game in Africa than our animal-trading firm could possibly move in a year. Something new was very much afoot, but we were going to have to wait a month or two to learn the details.

With several more cubs to rear, and night schedules of feeds again disrupting sleep, I was thrown into a treadmill of work as soon as I got back to The Pheasantry. So much so that I forgot most of the time that I was pregnant. Although it was my first, it would be just another birth among so many.

Marquis, too, was lumped in again with the others for feeding, loving and playing, and he resented it a little at first. Indeed, having had me so much to himself at Castle Combe he had become just a little spoiled, as any child would. But his good nature overcame all, and we soon settled down to the crazy life at home that had been interrupted by the film. Mercifully, we cannot foresee what is to come, but are permitted to live each moment as it is given to us. And 'living each moment' was routine at The Pheasantry.

In order to be ready at all times for television and film requirements, I am in the habit of shuttling various trained animals, from our zoo at Southampton to The Pheasantry and back, to keep them up to date in their tricks. It would be quite impossible to have them *all* around me all the time. Thirty is about the top limit in numbers I can cope with at home, even with the help of grooms, staff and the family. Besides, the grown animals like the life at Southampton and the daily contact with the public it brings.

Despite the other demands, on our return from the *Dr Dolittle* saga, I had decided it was time to give a refresher course to Hereward the snake, who had been transferred to Southampton when the first cubs were being reared. Hereward is a fully-grown Indian rock-python. He is about twenty feet long, and, as they grow about a foot a year for the first half of their lives, he must be about twenty years of age and should live to forty with any luck.

Pythons are quite intelligent and have individual personalities, believe it or not, good or bad as the case may be. Hereward is rather sweet and disposed to be friendly towards me, which is just as well considering his size and strength. Despite their intelligence, pythons do not really learn tricks. What happens is that they get used to being handled by one person to the point that they can be manipulated freely and, if well fed, will not bite, crush or strangle the handler. A python's bite, although not poisonous, is most painful, for they have long, needle-sharp teeth. And they can choke or squeeze a person to death in no time.

A handler can make a great show of wrestling with a python or pretending to be crushed or strangled by it. The way to make a python let go, by the way, if it forgets itself and means to choke you, is to bend its tail back sharply. But, as this is also the way to kill it, moderation has to be exercised, even in panic.

Being literally cold-blooded, snakes take on the temperature of wherever they happen to be. The hotter they are, the livelier they are. If you want a really quiet snake, keep it cool.

Anyway, I had Hereward at home for a bit while he got used to me again as his friend. At nights I would tie him up in a large sack downstairs where he would sleep quite happily.

One night I was just getting off to sleep between Marquis and Roger, after feeding a couple of cubs, when my feet touched something clammy, warm and rough. I leapt out of bed, while my two faithful he-men slept on. It was Hereward. He had escaped from his sack, followed me upstairs and sneaked into the bottom of the bed (if a twenty foot by four inch body can be said to sneak). I scolded him and returned him to his sack. I don't mind a lion in my bed but a python as well is a bit much.

Hereward was not very popular with the other animals. He never showed any signs of aversion, nor did he ever threaten to attack them, but he was disliked. They all kept well out of his way. The young lions would squat back on their haunches, hissing, if he was anywhere near them. Brave though they were in other ways, Lisa and Sheba were particularly petrified of him.

Even more interesting was the behaviour of Sammy, a pet

chameleon, who sometimes travelled around on my shoulder in summer, keeping me free from flies! If Sammy was within twenty feet of Hereward, he would puff himself up, inflating his airsacks, his swivelling eyes working overtime, until I removed him from the scene. Sammy's sudden transformations from slimness to grossness in his presence seemed to puzzle and even frighten Hereward. I suppose in some parts of the world snakes eat chameleons, and this is borne out by the fact that Sammy tended to puff himself up in the presence of even a garden hose, indicating that there is no hypnotism involved. But Sammy's apprehension was uncalled for, as it happened. Hereward, in truth, is only interested in whole English rabbits, which he swallows in gulps and digests over a period of days. (Pythons have to be treated with care and quiet after feeding, by the way, or they may eject the whole contents of their stomachs. They are extraordinarily sensitive, and the slightest disturbance can lead to regurgitation.)

Nor did visitors to The Pheasantry, generally speaking, favour my occasional preoccupations with snakes. I find this rather strange. Almost anyone can be persuaded to fondle a half-grown lion or tiger, given encouragement. But most people will run a mile when they see a snake on the loose. To many human beings, a snake is not just another member of the animal kingdom. It is a repugnant creature apart—a Something to be avoided and not ever to be talked about let alone handled. The most rational and calm beings can become madly hysterical in the presence of even a grass snake.

I have to hide Hereward away if I know certain of the female staff are likely to be around because they faint on the spot at the sight of him. Some people even react with horror and disgust when they see *pictures* of snakes, or when the word is spoken. Me? I rather like them, and although I do not care to have Hereward wrapped around my feet in bed, he fascinates and pleases me. But, when I get resentful of other people's reactions, I have to remind myself that I am just as irrational about insects. To each his private revulsion, I suppose.

When you have wild and tame animals around the house,

the senses are ever alert to danger signals which can warn of physical and emotional upsets or disturbances in behaviour patterns . . . and, more importantly, the threat of illness. Not only the eye and the ear but also the nose must play an active part.

In mammals, in particular, the whole body is an open book to be read by those who care enough to have learned to know how. Every aspect, from the way the hair lies to the position of the tip of the tail, has its special meaning. Smells, facial play and the pitch of cries can all contain important messages.

Healthy young animals eat when they are hungry and sleep when they are tired. Their resistance to germs is less than that of adult animals, so they need protection against infectious diseases and nutritional disorders. Generally speaking, the sooner these are detected, and the sooner treatment can begin, the better. The best precautions are inoculations, attention to basic hygiene and to safety.

Within a week of our return from Castle Combe, all my senses told me that Marquis was sickening for something. And, equally, my eyes, ears and nose suggested that it was that most dreaded of cat diseases (equally hateful with wild or domestic animals because it is so often fatal), feline enteritis. But I resisted my instincts, partly because I knew he had been inoculated against it, as had all the cubs, and partly because I could not bear the thought of my darling being ill. The obvious is often the hardest to swallow.

But sure enough, he was off his food, his mouth was dribbling, his nose running, he was vomiting and the diarrhoea which had started would not be stemmed. I broke up a streptotriad tablet and gave him the required portion until the vet could reach us. Marquis went to sleep soon afterwards but was so restless and fitful that I sat with him, gently holding his damp paws.

The vet took one look and confirmed my worst suspicions. 'It's cat flu all right,' he said grimly, and adding nought for my consolation, went on, 'He probably caught it from one of those tabbies you've been leading around.' He had had to tend a few of the thirty cats, so he knew what I had been up to. As the penny dropped, and I realized that I had exposed Marquis unnecessarily to danger, I flushed with guilt. The moggies for the film had been rounded up from various sources, and I had had no proof that they had all been inoculated against feline enteritis. And domestic cats are notorious carriers of the disease.

On the other hand, I told myself, the vaccine in use then was not all that effective. Marquis was a case in point. He *had* been properly injected, but had still caught it.

I was very depressed for a few days. Marquis was desperately ill, with a high fever and was sick all the time. The inflammation in his intestines meant that he could not be fed normally, so he had to be drip fed. A big needle was inserted under his skin and a special gluconate solution, brought by the vet, was dripped in gradually as his body was able to accept it. Medicines had to be forced down his throat, a process that was painful for both of us, the more so as the illness was making him salivate constantly, like a pricked water-blister.

Too weak, after the first few awful days, to move around, Marquis lay in my bed, night and day, fatly wrapped in blankets, his beloved alarm clock beside him but no longer very effective, and hot-water bottles all around for his comfort. I remained with him, like a nurse, virtually all the time, often falling asleep in the chair by the bed, my thumb in his mouth to confirm to him he was still my baby. Cat flu cannot be passed to humans, so there was no danger to the little urchin now kicking merrily inside me.

I watched over Marquis, but was frustrated by being able to do so little to help him. I waited, scarcely daring to hope.

The vet was absolutely marvellous and attended Marquis twice a day, giving all the bedside-mannered attention a family doctor would give to a favourite patient.

Inevitably there were messes on the bed to be cleared up, for with enteritis, cats cannot control their bodily functions and, even with constant watching, it was not always possible to catch the moment of evacuation and get the newspapers under him in time. But I was far too sorry for him to be cross about this. I only wanted him to be well again.

Marquis's weight before his illness had been coming up to eighty pounds and he was about the size of Yula and Gipsy, our Alsatians. Now he was pining away to a bag-of-bones condition that was terribly distressing to see, his back now as thin and spindly as an eel-cage; his dilated nostrils gaping like badger holes.

There was a crisis point every day and each one was an agony because so few animals ever recover from cat flu. I would look at his eyes constantly, at the height of the fever, searching for a sign that we had together surmounted that day's obstacle, and receiving like manna the occasional sad adoring look.

And, in the long nights, I would look for the night light of his peaceful sleep to calm my fears . . . the reassuring shadows of his deeper breathing thrown across me for my comfort. Or he would shiver with fever and we would draw together, feeling primeval chills. At such times, it would seem to me that the sun was dying and that the wolves of the wilderness were gathering around us. Those terrible nights were seemingly never-ending, as though someone had stuffed all the clocks in the house with cottonwool.

One night, he gave a little rattle in his throat and so sure was I that his frail spirit was being summoned to an African Valhalla that I lifted him from the bed and walked about with him cradled in a blanket in my arms, crooning to him as to a baby, willing him not to leave us.

There were sunny days, of course, and the garden was a buzzing jungle of richness, with butterflies wafting on the golden air like spiced wafers, but while Marquis was on the threshold of death, nature's bounties were unreal and meaningless. My panting dogs and lions crouching in the shade of the trees knew that there was illness in the house and did not even call for me as they would do normally if their meals were delayed or if they felt it should be time for walks or play.

Marquis's eyes were sunk in his yellowish, churchyard-angel skull, like two deep and over-brilliant holes. He was pale, consumptive and frail as thistledown. Tufts of sweat-soaked hair were sticking from his dull coat, like frosted grass on a stone. A white glow surrounded him as from a daylight moon. I was often tight with dread as his pulse fluttered through a crisis.

Grey and unhappy-faced, he would be hot and cold in turn, teeth chattering, swaying uneasily in fresh fever, restless as though lying in a bed of thorns. I would mop his brow and rearrange his bedclothes for the hundredth time, as he lay in an evil swamp of sweat.

Somehow we weathered twenty days of delusions, acute dangers and turning points, as the sick blood roared in his veins and his body wasted away before my eyes, beautiful sometimes in its fragility. Often the vet would shake his head sadly, implying that he could not last another night. But he did and he did . . . And on the twenty-first day, after a crisis in which his body raged through the hot winds of Africa only to be swept into the bitter cold of an Arctic blizzard, I sensed a change. Secretly, silently, aided by unknown ancestral forces, he began to surface at last from the long delirium, climbing the steep hill back from the dead.

It was instant joy. His strained face broke momentarily into a little Cheshire-cat grin to tell me all was well and then, with the most profound feeling of peace, we both sank into the sweet serenity of natural, unfevered sleep.

The dramatic recovery took place on the morning of 22 September, 1966, when Marquis was just seven and a half months old. I rose late and the birth pains were on me. I packed quietly while Marquis slept on, weak but safely on the road back to lusty health. Late that afternoon Roger, who had always been by my side when I needed him over the long weeks of Marquis's illness, drove me to Salisbury where I had a private hospital room booked. The next morning my perfect baby boy was born, all nine pounds of him. I had booked privately to ensure that I would not get someone else's child by mistake—knowing full well the problems of having a lot of babies around the place. I need not have worried. David was the only baby delivered in the hospital at the time. They more or less tied me to my bed for the five

days they considered to be the absolute minimum time for a
mother to be kept in and then I fled back to The Pheasantry
where Marquis was recovering splendidly and where David
would have to take bottle-luck with a growing number of
young cubs from the reserve for his feed.

Chapter Nineteen

MORE EAST AFRICAN GAME
IN WILTSHIRE

On my first day home, the radio in the office bleeped a message that important visitors had arrived at Longleat and
would we rally round to escort them through the reserve. It
turned out to be King Bhumibol and Queen Sirikit of Thai-
land and two of their four children. They had been on a
private visit to friends in Somerset and had suddenly decided
to take in Longleat.

We put on our best bibs and tuckers and greeted the royal
party. The five cars were positively bristling with security
men as they entered the massive gates with their lion emblems.
But all went well until the convoy stopped to have a look at
the 'family' of lions in the Plains of Abraham section. These
consist of Abraham, Khan and 'the Jews'. Among 'the Jews'
is Solly, who has a particularly inquisitive nature and is not
averse to having an occasional nibble at a car. Knowing this,
Mike Lockyer was hovering nearby, in case of any mis-
behaviour.

The King was obviously enjoying himself and was pointing
out some of the animals' finer points to his beautiful young
Queen. Solly watched for a while and then approached the
car to have a closer look at what the people were up to.
Mike hovered nearby, knowing the occupants had their windows closed and were safe. Then he noticed the fluttering
flag on the bonnet of the King's car and, in a split second,
saw that Solly had noticed it, too. Aware that the lion was

likely to bite off the flag and its silver staff, and anxious to avoid such an insult, Mike leapt forward, resplendent in his 'white hunter' uniform, thrusting his gun between the lion and the car.

To say that his gesture was misunderstood, would be a major understatement. Before either he or Solly could make another move, the convoy had raced off at high speed and out of the park, as if the entire lion population was in pursuit. Apparently what had happened was that the security guards had thought Mike might assassinate the King and had put into operation the emergency 'scalded cat' operation pre-arranged for any such contingencies. They were half way back to Somerset before the rest of us could catch our breath.

By early October, the number of visitors was decreasing rapidly and it was time for Father to reveal his future plans and add still further to the complications of life at The Pheasantry. One morning he emerged from a huddle with Lord Bath to announce that further rapid expansion had been agreed. Exhausted though we were after the incredible events of the season, we sat quietly and listened. When Jimmy Chipperfield is in the saddle nobody dares to mention the height of the jumps!

The first ideas were to have hippos among the reeds in the lake and a colony of adult chimpanzees on the island. Boats would also be installed so that the public could observe more closely these un-English phenomena.

Again it was an imaginative idea. Nor was it an impractical one. Neither animal, in the full-grown state, was look-at-able to any extent in Europe. And few zoos have ever been able to breed chimps successfully because adult animals can seldom be retained.

At one time we had a hippo called Harry in our circus. My Uncle Dick had been mainly responsible for Harry's welfare, but other members of the family were able to take over when necessary. As my father outlined the hippo scheme for Long-leat, I was comforted in my remembrances of Harry as a very friendly animal. We had had him from the time he was a baby, and I had more or less grown up with him. He had been fed on hay, carrots, bran and oats, and had got through every bit as much in a day as an elephant. A special waggon had had to be created for him, with a built-in tank, into which he could submerge. He had loved human company and I had often been in the habit of visiting him for a chat.

Harry was not very bright, but otherwise was a real pet—all one and a half tons of him. He had liked to have his nose rubbed and his head stroked. The only trouble had been that, when you got tired and desisted, he would roar his displeasure in the most deafening way.

Many a time I had ridden on Harry's back around the circus compound. But in the ring he had only been hauled in with the giraffes as a spectacle, being too dumb to do tricks.

So, as my father talked, hippos did not loom large in my mind as a worry, although I had also seen them fighting amongst themselves in Africa.

Fully grown chimpanzees were another matter. I had also grown up with many chimps, but they had all been young ones. By the time they are about six years of age, they can have the strength of four men and can cause truly terrible injuries by biting with their sharp fangs.

Young chimps are marvellous fun and can learn endless routines. Among circus animals they are in a class by themselves. Circus people never refer to them as animals. They are always the lads, or the kids, or the boys. They are also among the most intelligent of animals. But the public would certainly have to be protected from adult chimpanzees, which can weigh more than the average man and which are given to sudden tantrums, dislikes and malicious villainies.

Father's answer, of course, was that chimpanzees have a natural fear of water. and the island was, therefore, an ideal setting, giving them plenty of space to live and to breed, and yet ensuring that they could not harm the visitors.

So it was that, in the winter of 1966-67, we set to with wardens and estate workers and cleared much of the island of nettles, brambles and other 'hides'. We also built two draught-proof huts. And we generally made the island ready for animal-occupation.

As no one wanted them, adult chimpanzees were fairly easy to obtain. The first four adults, Max, Alby, Simon, and

Mona, all good specimens, were soon bought from zoos which were about to dispose of them anyway. Temporary accommodation had meanwhile been arranged for them near the Pets' Corner while we thought up ways of transferring them to the island.

Simply crating them and shipping them by rowing boat was considered but discarded as being too cumbersome and hazardous. So the vet was called in and each chimp was knocked unconscious by a tranquillizing drug, injected by means of a dart fired from a cross-bow. We then lifted them bodily, one of us at each limb, and one by one their large insensate frames were rowed across the lake.

Two chimps were put in each hut, and, when they had recovered from the effects of the drug, they were allowed to explore the island. This they did with great thoroughness— examining every detail meticulously . . . so much so that it was two days before they could be coaxed back into the huts —and this was mid-winter. Eventually, a drill was worked out in which they had their evening meals in the hut and were then locked in for the night.

Meanwhile, on the shore of the lake, a huge hippo enclosure had been created. And, soon after the arrival of the first chimps, three hippos rolled up the drive by the lake. The extent of 'hippo-land' was about an acre—half of it water and half mud. This gave them much more freedom than they had had before in Hanover Zoo or in our zoo at Southampton.

All was ready in the early spring and the opening ceremony, at which Lord Bath's daugher, Lady Silvy, launched a boat named after her, created another flush of welcome publicity for Longleat. Such, indeed, was the public response, that, by Easter, it was obvious that a second boat would have to be ordered. This one was ready for Whitsun, and was named *Mary Rose* after me! Like the *Lady Silvy*, the *Mary Rose* featured a colourful canopy and awnings. It also, appropriately, boasted a rearing horse figurehead, instead of the dragon's head of the other boat. Both figureheads were the work of a designer friend of the Marquess, Mano Hornak.

During the winter we had also erected a low fence across

the lower valley section of the lion reserve and had fenced off about twenty-seven acres, containing two sleeping huts. These were prepared specially for our most promising breeding group. This consisted of Leo (father of Marquis) together with his harem—Sneaky, Chaser and Stumpy. They were a happy family, with the possible exception of Stumpy, who had an inferiority complex about her stature and occasionally fell out with the other two lionesses.

The experiment worked well and during April both Sneaky and Chaser had litters—of four and three cubs respectively.

As it turned out, and I could have predicted this, Sneaky was an excellent mother in every way and nothing could have taken her four lovely cubs away from her.

Chaser, on the other hand, was as wayward as they come, and this, too, was in character. As I watched from a patrol vehicle, as near as I dared go in the circumstances, Chaser 'dropped' one cub on the verandah of the hut she was occupying. Almost instantly, she rose from the spot, walked inside the hut and had two more babies in the straw. She remained with the two in the warm and never went back for the little one on the verandah. If she had felt for it, she would have taken it inside, gently carrying it in her mouth. But she did not want it. So I took it home to The Pheasantry, another of the many orphans, to feed and rear.

This baby was a female and, from the start, she was irresistible—sweet-natured, docile and full of fun. We called her Zena, and after eight weeks in our home, I took her to Pets' Corner at Longleat, where she was an outstanding attraction.

Sneaky and Chaser were typical of the 'sister acts' I have encountered so often among lions. As soon as Chaser rejoined the pride, with her two remaining cubs, Sneaky showed as much affection for them as for her own four. Chaser took less and less interest in the babies, as time went on, but she did take turns occasionally of suckling any or all of the six cubs. Such is life in an animal harem!

Leo, who was husband to both lionesses, was unusual in that he was a marvellous father. Noble and yet tolerant, he did not wander off in pursuit of other lionesses after the births, as so many do. Instead, he played games with the cubs for many weeks, allowing them to climb all over him as he lay on the grass; cuffing them affectionately when they bit him; and generally playing the benign king and the proud father. This was a joy to see.

When the cubs got to seven weeks, and were ready for meat, he resignedly let them nibble succulent bits off the joints he was eating, and, believe me, this is a most unusual thing for lion fathers to do . . . or human fathers for that matter. When the BBC television unit arrived, soon after this, to film their first programme in the lion reserve, they were able to get some splendid pictures of Leo walking about with a large bone in his mouth . . . and at each end of the bone a cub was dangling, hanging on for grim life to tasty morsels of meat still adhering to the bone!

During that summer of 1967, Leo, Sneaky, Chaser and Stumpy, with the six cubs that remained with them, were undoubtedly the most photographed pride of lions in the world.

As the babies were among the first we had successfully reared in the open, I spent many an hour observing them and keeping a motherly eye on them. As it turned out, when they were big enough to feed on their own, they became a source of some anxiety, because they began to wander off, exploring the reserve and taking a look at the other animals. Mike Lockyer and his men would search, of an evening, for missing 'children' in the undergrowth, because we felt it wise, in those experimental days, to shut up the cubs in one of the huts at night with their mothers.

One evening, try as we might, we just could not locate one of the cubs. I scarcely slept, imagining all sorts of horrors. And, the next morning at dawn, we resumed the search. Goodness knows where he was, because it was not until that afternoon, nearly twenty-four hours after he had been missed, that the little lion was seen strolling up the road among the cars, sweetly and innocently heading for 'home' in the hut, acting for all the world as if he was a child returning from school. I did not worry half so much thereafter, but I still wonder where he went and what he was up to for a whole day and night.

By this time the thirteen Ethiopian lions were out of quarantine and established in the park, as were several of the cubs I had reared in The Pheasantry. My breeding operations were also going well, and it was time to think of making a business of the surplus lions we would be producing.

We had received many enquiries at The Pheasantry for cubs and young lions. So, when Sneaky and Chaser's offspring were about six months old and in robust health, it seemed safe to begin dealing in lions again with sales as well as purchases.

Among the more urgent requests for breeding stock we had received was one from a zoo in Ibadan, Nigeria, for a young lioness. This stirred my imagination. Nigeria was once extensively peopled by lions in the wild. Now, apparently, it has very few, even in captivity. As soon as the second season at Longleat was over, I crated a really beautiful, Longleat-bred, young lioness and sent her by air to Ibadan, where she settled quickly and is now producing cubs.

I felt that it was important and worthwhile that the first exported Lion of Longleat should go to Africa and should breed there.

Chapter Twenty

THE LION AND THE HORSE

Although now huge, Marquis continued to share our bed and, in many ways, dominate our lives. By comparison, our real baby, David John Cawley, was so little trouble that he fitted into the scheme of things quietly and naturally from the start —happy, unspoiled and gregarious.

One of the problems with Marquis was that he had become a very deep sleeper, and, by the time he woke up in the mornings, he was always more than ready to go to the toilet —which, for him, was now the garden. The result was that one or other of us, whoever rose first, would have to get dressed quickly and quietly, ready to attend to Marquis's needs the moment his eyelids fluttered. Over and over again Roger would have to stop half way through a shave, or before it, while still in pyjamas—or I would be caught with only my nightie on—to rush one large lion down the stairs and out through the french windows. He was then doing about a gallon of widdle a time and his favourite place for it was a Wistaria bush in a corner of the garden. How that shrub is still alive, I will never know. It must come from a very hardy plant strain!

By the time David was a few months old he had no fear at all of any of the animals, nor had they of him. This is not to say that there were no disagreements; there were occasional periods of tears all round, as well as of laughter.

Charles, a splendid young chimpanzee, and J-J, a baby gorilla, had by this time joined the throng in The Pheasantry and were virtually regarded by David and by us as his brothers. Sean, the Great Dane, was also a particular favourite, to be bossed and made use of. David seemed pleased enough to have us as parents, but he was mainly absorbed in a world of young animals of whom he never tired.

What with one thing and another, David was seven months old before we found a free Sunday to get him christened. But when it did happen—at St Michael and All Angels Church, Bassett, Southampton—it was unusual in that it was attended by a lion and a lord: Marquis and the Marquess of Bath.

A nanny also became a necessity to give David somebody to turn to in needs and emergencies during our many other involvements. But she had to be a very special nanny and certainly not a genteel-type lady, used to steering posh prams between stately willows in Kensington Gardens. Qualities over and above the usual call of duty were demanded, including adaptability. The sort of things she would have to cope with would include sorting out a playpen full of lion cubs which were being chastised by one small boy; or making an instant decision on whether David had had more rides on the tricycle than Charles the Chimp. Somehow a twenty-year-old girl, Frances Robinson, took all this on and more. She was a real character—a most unusual girl; but that is what you have to be in a home like ours!

She even had to help hold the chains when press pictures were taken of David 'playing' with a fully grown tiger (Kumar, of course) and an apparently fully grown lion (Marquis) when David was only about six weeks old. They were excellent photographs of the three in David's bed. What they did not show was Frances and yours truly crouched under the bed holding the animals' chains.

In fact, David was not allowed to play with the *larger* animals until he was about four months old. Then he made up for lost time by knocking them about something cruel!

There were so many animals around the house by this time that local GPO service engineers downed tools and refused to help us any more unless they got 'danger money'. The trouble was that the cubs, aided betimes by boy, chimp and gorilla, had found a new sport—chewing through telephone wires. After several calls in which they had to repair the damage while their ankles were being nibbled by the occasional leopard, and while little lions pulled their tool bags about for fun, they 'blacked' The Pheasantry. This was serious. We live by the telephone to some extent. So we had more or less to get down on our knees and plead with them to help just once more. We undertook to lock up all the animals while they were working. And we hit on the brilliant idea of having all the wires slung around the tops of the walls instead of around the skirting boards, so that the cubs could not get at them. Adaptability is all!

I had added a black panther, Phoenix, to my private collection by this time, so a run had to be made for him at the back of the henhouse. The hens had some narrow squeaks from Phoenix, but soon learned to peck just out of range of his claws and teeth. And, instead of tomatoes, I had a couple of giant tortoises in the greenhouse.

I took in another elephant, too, about this time. Her name was Wamba. Richard had caught her in Africa and she was aged about four when I installed her in the garage at The Pheasantry. Wamba is a 'natural' in every way—marvellous in television and films. She is brighter than most; marvellous in traffic; and she knows all the tricks—begging, rearing, standing on her head. I had first ridden an elephant act in the circus when I was twelve, so I knew how to put her through her paces.

But, above all else, I had never had an animal (lion or otherwise) as intelligent and tractable as Marquis, so I had begun seriously to train him from the age of about a year, knowing that he would be outstanding in films, television commercials, fashion plates and so on. He was by now a splendid-looking specimen, weighing nearly two hundred pounds, regarded as fully grown by strangers but less than two-thirds the weight and size he would eventually reach. His second teeth were now complete, giving him a grin or grimace that could be awesome to behold. When he felt playful, he could knock Roger over with one uninhibited swipe from an enormous paw. Fairly dark in colour, he was growing a splendid black mane and under-mane, with a bushy, woolly black tuft on the end of his long tail. He was sharp-eyed now and somewhat haughty.

Apart from the fact that it provides an income for their owners, training is important and necessary for captive and semi-captive animals for two very good reasons. In their daily lives in the wild, their two chief preoccupations would be (1) constant alertness against enemies and (2) the implacable necessity of killing for food. When the need for these activities is removed, periods of emptiness are created which can lead, in extreme cases, to an awful boredom or to the development of wilful and perverse traits. In the old days of small, barred cages and gloomy dens, this unnatural inactivity could lead to a morbidness that was most distressing to see. Having grown up in the circus, I have always understood an animal's need for occupation or substitute-activity, and our wild creatures never had to resort to the endless walking in circles, the neuroses, the self-mutilation and so on of the deprived animals in the more miserable of zoos.

All our animals received daily training and exercise which they enjoyed repeating and expanding upon. They always had something to occupy their minds. And they were well housed. Such is the case, too, with our zoo animals at Southampton and Plymouth, and even more so at The Pheasantry. They are allowed to express themselves in behavioural and 'party' tricks to a greater or lesser degree, according to their needs.

Different species are extraordinarily dissimilar in these respects. Some have great need of activity; others very little. With some, if you do not play with them or allow them to entertain enough they will make up games and performances of their own. This is particularly true of apes in general and chimps in particular (witness the tea-parties they enjoy so much). It is also to be found strongly among seals, porpoises and dolphins. Many predators, too, like balls to play with, as do certain ungulates; and many birds enjoy mirrors, stones, or even simple toys.

Where zoo or park animals are kept in herds, they invariably provide their own specific games at will. Antelopes at Longleat play the same sort of 'king of the castle' games as schoolchildren. My elephants like to have something of their own to play with in their quarters—like a large tree root or an old wheel. This is to them what Marquis's alarm clock is to him, except that they toss their 'toy' about for fun.

Such games are an excellent therapeutic means for filling the gap in movement and activity brought about by captivity. But more serious training towards the specific aim of entertainment and/or education is possible with and beneficial to a great many wild animals. Often play imperceptibly merges into training practice in the sense that training is really a sort of disciplined play.

The discipline is the thing—especially with animals that are stronger than their trainers—and most enjoy the discipline, together with the obedience it implies.

Sometimes I look at my wiry but slight body in the mirror (with its thin skin, fragile bones and relatively weak powers) and wonder how I can possibly master anthropoid apes, larger predators and ungulates, all so much stronger than I can ever hope to be. But I manage to school wild and tame animals, individually and collectively, every day, in a great variety of ways. I have trained liberty horses and ponies and high school horses to perform the most intricate manoeuvres or to 'count' and 'spell'. I have taught chimpanzees to ride bicycles, walk on stilts, dance and do gymnastics. I have put lions and tigers through flaming hoops. And so on . . .

Good training is disciplined play. Both play and training brighten the daily lives of the animals concerned. There is no cruelty involved. Any trainer who was cruel to an animal would be out of business quicker than a confectioner who sold poisoned sweets.

An animal's performance is based very largely on habit, and this is true of wild animals as of domestic ones. Cows coming in for milking soon get to know their individual stalls and a brewery dray horse quickly learns the stopping places without prompting. Similarly, trained chimps *insist* on sitting down to tea as soon as a table is laid.

In preparing any young animal of the cat family for commercial or entertainment work, my early disciplines have been simple and fairly constant. First, he would be got used to a collar, from about six weeks, having been brought up as a 'child' in the household, probably from birth. He would also have been taken around in his basket (by car, bus or train) to 'open' fêtes and attend other such public events. He would make appearances at Pets' Corner at Longleat. He would be introduced to first a lead and then a chain, for about ten weeks, and would be taken for walks twice a day to get used to being led. He would learn to lie down, stand up, walk on and walk off, to cues. During all such occasions, he would gradually get used to people outside the family circle and would therefore behave well in the sometimes crowded and busy atmosphere of a studio or location. And when he was due to appear before the cameras, he would have been taken in advance to the shooting floor to see and get to know the equipment so that sudden noise and movements would not frighten him. It is important that he should see and hear my cues to him whatever is going on around.

All these simple disciplines are fairly common to all of us who train animals professionally, and, although he was very specially precious to me, they applied as much to Marquis as to any of my cubs in his maturing months. He made his appearances at Pets' Corner on Sundays. He travelled around in the front of my 1100 or in the back of my Cortina estate-car. He opened shops and galas. He walked around in traffic and among pedestrians in busy streets. He switched on the 1966 Christmas lights at Bath with Lord Bath. He appeared in simple commercials for Booths Gin and was given a magnificent hand-made collar by the firm. In brief, he lived the full life of a normal lion from the East now living in the West! And he was by now receiving a considerable amount of 'pop star' fan-mail.

But I had, as I say, higher ambitions for Marquis. Just before his first birthday I began preparing him to do a trick with one of my horses, which is outside the natural order of things and which is against every instinct of lion or horse.

The basic idea was to teach the two hundred pound lion to leap on and off a horse's back and ride there.

The horse I had chosen for the experiment was Jarro, a Spanish stallion of fifteen hands. First I got them used to one another. I would take Marquis into the stable when I was grooming the horse and all the while I would talk to both of them, letting them know that we belonged to each other, all three.

Next, I took to chaining Marquis near the horse in the stable and leaving them together for long periods to get used to each other. They could not touch but they were close enough to become familiar with each other's smells, sounds and moods. Gradually, in a sweet and rather noble way, they became friends.

Separately, I would then introduce them to individual aspects of the 'act' I hoped they would do together. This required a great deal of time and patience.

Jarro was an exceptionally good-natured and well-disciplined horse. I would trot him round with a small dog on his back until he got used to this and would then introduce larger dogs to the routine until Jarro was quite accustomed to a heavy Alsatian jumping on top of him, riding there, and jumping off again.

Meanwhile, I was teaching Marquis to jump on and off circus pedestals, the height of which I gradually increased until they were the same height as the horse.

Next, I would trot Jarro past while Marquis was jumping on the pedestal. This would go on day after day, as I talked to both, until they were thoroughly used to each other's movements and performances. Gradually, Marquis would learn to touch the padded blanket on the horse's back with his paw as it passed and would be able to judge the distance between them.

When the big day came for Marquis's first leap into the saddle, as it were, the event was almost an anti-climax. He did it so perfectly first time, and Jarro reacted so quietly and well, that I could scarcely believe it was happening. I had intended that Marquis should first place two paws on Jarro's back, preparatory to his first leap. Instead, he jumped straight on to the blanket and sat there quietly. On and off Marquis went . . . on and off, as Jarro trotted along. They were my friends. They had confidence in me. They would do anything I asked.

The entire experiment had taken less than four months.

It was a marvellous feeling to have pulled it off—like flying to the moon. I was breaking new ground in animal training. But I had always known that Marquis was superior to any other lion and would do anything within reason I required of him.

Some time after this, BBC producer Derek Burrel-Davis came down to 'recce' the place and see how he could best present the Lions of Longleat in a series of television shows. He decided that Marquis should be the star and he featured the Jarro act in the first programme. It went without a hitch. But afterwards, as a warning to others who might be tempted to try something similar with less intelligent and trustworthy animals, I teased Marquis with a chunk of meat and he went for me. The one time you must keep away from a lion, even my Marquis, is when he is feeding. And you must always be watchful, even with the lion you love.

The *Sunday Mirror* was one of many papers to be tremendously impressed. It said:

> The BBC must be wondering why they ever bought that ludicrous load of 'darkest Africa' animal hokum, Daktari, from Hollywood, when they could have made a much better series in darkest Wiltshire . . .

The Daktari household of Mary and Roger Cawley proved so engaging that Burrel-Davis devoted half the programme to them because 'it was all so natural and marvellous'.

Since the British are known to be mad about animals, why didn't the BBC think of it long ago?

Sunday Mirror, 11 November, 1967.

Alas, although all the television companies import American wild animal series galore and buy up animal programmes from all parts of the world, any work they have asked me to do for them has been occasional and spasmodic. I *could* create an all-British series for them that would make Daktari a back number. But so far I have not been asked.

Chapter Twenty-One

GAME FOR A NEW DEVELOPMENT

While I had been training Marquis, I had also been considerably occupied with matters connected with the reserve and other Chipperfield enterprises. The first season of hippos and chimps in Half-Mile Pond and its island was proving a great additional attraction, and it was clear that Lord Bath no longer had to worry about where the next tin of termite-spray was coming from. The lions had driven the wolves from the stately doors and other animals would soon consolidate the position. Indeed, a Mexican gentleman walked up to the Marquess in the park one day and offered him a million pounds cash for Longleat and its attractions. 'I would not sell for ten million,' was the no-nonsense reply.

The chimp family on the island, now called Man-Ape Island, had been renamed Harold, George, Jim, Barbara and Edward.

WHITEHALL STUNNED, said the headlines, and the story

began 'Day-trippers throw apples, bananas to well-known figures on Wiltshire island . . .' It was all good clean fun. 'If anyone wants to read anything political into this, they can,' said ex-MP Lord Bath spiritedly.

The personalities suited the names very well. As the *Daily Mirror* reporter described them, 'George claps his hands, cries his love call and tries to monopolize everything. Harold is fairly mild. Jim is the largest—big, heavy and cumbersome; jovial and ferocious by turns. Barbara is the oldest but is very sexy. Edward smiles an awful lot; at the slightest excuse he pulls up his top lip and grins . . .'

The five celebrities had been provided with rope climbing frames and were putting on their vote-catching shows several times a day. The fifty-six seater, gold-painted 'stately barges' (based on the design for the royal barges for which Handel wrote his 'Water Music') took hundreds of visitors on half-hour trips on the lake, and the chimps, soon learning that food was likely to be thrown from the boats, geared their attention-attracting antics to this, to the delight of the passengers.

The primeval-looking hippos, too—Manfred, Arnold and Freda—were a great attraction, especially when Lord Bath chose to ride one while dressed in the cowboy gear he had acquired when he rode the ranges of Texas as a young man.

Soon after this we introduced nine sea-lions to the lake (shipped from California in a wet-tank truck) and they too met with immediate success as they followed the barges and leapt for fish supplied by us and thrown to them by the passengers, catching the silver morsels in the air, like Dexter or Engineer.

Like chimps, seals are great mimics. They soon worked out tricks of their own to entertain the visitors in return for the food, and their frantic barking added yet another alien but exciting sound to Longleat.

Battles soon developed between the seals and the chimps for food thrown from the boats near the water's edge at the island.

Inevitably, a member of the unpredictable public provided us with a fright one day when a man reached out too far in throwing a fish to a seal at the back of the *Mary Rose* barge and fell in beside it. The staff would soon have had him out except that for some inane reason he immediately struck out for the island which was quite near. The crew of the barge fortunately acted quickly and yanked him out with a boat hook or he would have been torn apart by the chimpanzees.

We now purchased another chimp, Sally, from Paignton Zoo and set about turning the island population into a breeding colony—something that had never been tried before in this way in Britain.

In other ways, plans were moving forward at a frantic pace as Father got the taste of unbridled success. He had been travelling the world for some months, setting up deals in other countries and shipping animals to Britain for future use. Richard, too, had been travelling and trapping wild animals.

Richard, in fact, was now in America, where Father had set up a partnership deal to open a reserve (on the lines of Longleat but larger) on a 640 acre estate at Royal Palm Beach West, in Florida, at the modest cost of one and a half million pounds! As it was much cheaper to ship animals from England (even by air freight) than to buy them in the States, we became frantically involved in organizing animal exports for a time and we even sent one of our two elephants to Florida. In all, over 100 animals were involved—many lions, elephants, rhinos and giraffes.

Another problem then arose. I had been invited to attend the opening of the Palm Beach park and to appear on a number of television programmes, panel games and interview shows in New York and Florida. Obviously, I was expected to appear with a stately animal and Marquis was the natural and desirable choice. I went through hell worrying about whether to take him or not, because he would have to go into quarantine again on his return. I finally decided against it, after searching my heart and deciding that I could not possibly do it to him (or was it to us?).

Instead, I cheated a little. I arranged to pick up one of our lions, Tasha, in America, and I pretended it was Marquis, the now-famous Longleat lion. Among the TV shows I appeared in was 'To Tell The Truth' in which I won sixty pounds, which came in useful. Tasha behaved splendidly, we got a tremendous amount of publicity and the new park was an instant success.

As soon as I could, I got back to The Pheasantry and found, sure enough, that Marquis had been off his food and pining. He heard my car before anyone and had to be let off his chain to greet me or he would have done himself an injury.

He was now so big that he had to spend much of his time in one of the garages in the yard. A mesh panel had been inserted in the door so that he could look out. But, in fact, he had been on a running wire in the garden the afternoon I returned and when he was released he leaped over the garden gate as if it was a low hurdle, simply flew to my car and had soaked me with his tongue before I could move. When I did manage to get out, he had his front paws round my neck and I had to walk him backwards in that position (taller than me) into the house before he would believe that I was back for good and was not going to desert him again.

My son David was far less concerned or interested. He did give me a peck and then went off to play with Charles and J-J. Marquis refused to leave my side.

A photographic fashion session had been laid on for early the following morning in the park, featuring Marquis. The girls were two of the world's top models. They were showing new 'jungle and fantasy' prints in natural surroundings. It was a super idea, or rather it would have been had the girls not been scared stiff of Marquis from the moment the cameras were set up in the woods near the house.

My lion was so pleased to have me home he scarcely noticed they were there. If he did notice, they bored him . . . which was certainly flattering to me! All he wanted to do was squat near by giving me welcoming, loving looks. But the models were petrified of him. He only had to flick his tail, or raise a paw to scratch his mane, or move to make himself more comfortable, or even yawn, and they took to their heels and headed for the nearest bushes. The more they ran, the longer it would take to set up the next picture. And conversely, the longer it took to set up the next picture, the more restless Marquis would become (wanting only to get back to The Pheasantry and hear about my trip). It was a vicious circle, I can tell you.

The photographer was trying to achieve a carefully staged savagery, to show off the splendid outfits which featured larger-than-life floral and butterfly designs, with gigantic flowers, herbs and exotic birds expressed in very vivid native colours. But such was the lack of 'cool' on the part of the girls that it took two whole days to complete the session instead of the few hours originally allocated. This caused many added problems for me and it made Marquis very fed up indeed . . . which added to the fear . . . which added to the time and the problems . . . Phew! Talk about cat-walks!

It was a fairly frantic week. The following day, Marquis was persuaded to sit at the controls of a new Cortina Lotus at its press presentation. And later the same week a new anti-cat-flu vaccine, FEV, was launched at Longleat, with Marquis featured as a 'typical' patient. As booster shots of what seemed to be a vastly improved preparation were injected in his shoulder, I could not help thinking back and wishing it had been available a year earlier. The dose for a lion, by the way, is five times as much as for a domestic cat. It is regrettable, I feel, that only about 60,000 of Britain's millions of pet cats are inoculated each year against this scourge of feline enteritis. In my book, it should be obligatory.

Darting techniques, in anaesthetizing large wild animals, had also been vastly improved and we had acquired special capture-pistols for firing the darts instead of the rather hit-and-miss cross-bows we had employed earlier. They were soon needed when Nigel. a huge lion scarred from old glories, and a most successful father, got a thorn in his foot. I knew him well and tried several times to approach him but the pain was apparently too great for him to be handled by anyone. Thinking back to my schooldays this made me feel rather inadequate for once. as I recalled how 'seeing the lion in great pain, Androcles forgot his terror and went forward. A great thorn had got into the paw, cutting it and making it swell. And Androcles drew out the thorn with a quick movement. pressed the swelling and stopped the flow of blood.

Relieved of pain, the grateful lion limped out of the cave . . .'

Ah well! Maybe lions were more understanding in those days. Nigel did not want to know me. Nor did he want to know the vet. So we called in Father, the best shot in the family, and he knocked out the large lion with one carefully aimed dart . . . although, of course, we had to wait some time for him to become fully unconscious. The vet then found the thorn still imbedded in one of Nigel's front paws, which was badly inflamed. He took the thorn out, and gave the deep-sleeping lion an antibiotic injection. When Nigel came to several hours later he seemed to have a bit of a headache, but his paw healed quickly and he was soon romping around happily with his wives.

At Whitsun, more people than ever turned up in the rain at Longleat and again there were incredible traffic problems. Thousands of people were turned away, as police forced them into *any* lanes or minor roads, away from the jammed highway; but 60,000 nevertheless managed to see the lions and another 7,000 sailed among the seals, hippos and chimps.

Some of the Longleat lions had been sent to America and fresh acclimatized stock had been brought to England from Sweden. There were sixteen of these in all—eight males, four females and four cubs—and we were able to quarantine them in special quarters, where they could be seen, at Longleat, instead of having to stage them through a zoo. They had lived in even colder conditions in Sweden than had ours at Longleat, and it was fascinating to note that their coats were longer and shaggier.

A large cold-room had also been established by now beside The Pheasantry so that we could cope with the vast and increasing quantities of meat and fish that were required each week. In order to keep up quality and quantity we were forced to place orders farther and farther afield and were now getting some of our supplies from as far away as Weston-super-Mare.

Shortly after Whitsun, an important hush-hush cargo arrived by ship at Avonmouth and we were all there to meet it. This consisted of twenty-two elegant-looking and rare Rothschild giraffes (worth £1,800 each) which Father had shipped from Uganda and which were immediately taken, by waiting lorries, to Plymouth Zoo to begin their quarantine. They were to be part of the largest giraffe herd outside Africa, which Father was proposing to introduce, with other animals, into a great new East African Game Reserve he was secretly scheduling for 1968, next to the lion park at Longleat.

The idea was to create an open safari parkland (well stocked with East African animals) around which families could picnic in the open—free of charge and restrictions—before driving through the lion reserve.

In addition to the herd of 'nature's skyscrapers', we intended to introduce zebras, gemsbock gazelles and ostriches, together with crowned cranes, vultures, storks (flown in from Spain) and other bird life. These were being rounded up in Europe and other parts of the world.

The vultures would be particularly welcome, from our point of view, because crows had become a major problem at feeding time in the lion park. I suppose you could call crows 'English vultures'. But they are so ugly, compared to African vultures, and are such untidy feeders as they part-scavenge the left-over meat when the lions have had their fill. The public did not like to see the crows at work, so we had to have them scared away and had to do the clearing up after feeding-time ourselves, as we had from the start, for reasons of hygiene as well as of aesthetics.

The ever-increasing length of the grass in the lion reserve was also becoming a problem, as it was preventing the lions being seen properly. In earlier years it had been kept down by deer, but were we to put deer back, it might for a time be possible to view the lions better but in due course the deer would disappear . . . down the predators' throats! So old-fashioned but safer methods had to be employed. Bronzed, self-reliant, God-fearing farm workers under the guardian-ship of armed white hunters, sliced away among the lions, with the grace of fencing-masters, their scythes and sickles (oiled, wrapped and put away at the end of each day) honed on whetstones to the sharpness of razors; their two-pint tea cans glinting in the sun; their Wiltshire pork sausages and pies wrapped in plastic but carried in old-style red bandana handkerchiefs, like the one Lord Bath invariably features in his top pocket. I found it refreshing and relaxing to be amongst them, as their arms swung in unison, decapitating buttercups, sweeping the seed puff-clocks off dandelions, and swinging among hay-makers in the jungle of uneven green lion park, previously cropped for centuries by native animals.

Later a tractor with trailer was called in to move the lush and sweet-smelling hay (which I would make good use of for my horses) and swathes flew from the fork-ends to land in great heaps on the trailer, festooning it like a Tahitian straw roof.

At the end of June, in continuingly beautiful weather, *Life* magazine did a major feature on the lions (starring Lord Bath and Marquis descending the grand staircase at Longleat House) and in the course of an excellent story, which brought us many interesting letters from zoologists throughout the world, described his lordship as 'the mad Marquess with the noble zoo'. And about the same time my lion, together with several of my other animals, was featured in the James Bond extravaganza *Casino Royale*, which was part-filmed in the grounds and around the house. Marquis was also asked, as special guest, when the International Lions' Club (a benevolent institution) held a function at Frome. Complete issues of children's comics were devoted to his doings.

So obvious was the success of the Longleat project by now that countless suggestions were being made to us by entrepreneurs and businessmen anxious to ride on our backs, as it were. One of the more interesting and intriguing came from an old friend of mine (from my horse-breeding and showing days), Luis Gordon, a Spanish thirty-four-year-old director of a leading sherry-shipping firm. He suggested a bullfight at Longleat, tied to a sherry-drinking fiesta. Nothing came of it. Lord Bath put it this way, 'The sherry-drinking is cruelty to human beings, and that's all right. But the bull-fighting is cruelty to animals, so it's no go.'

Chapter Twenty-Two

SURPRISE FOR A POACHER

The Pheasantry, the large house we live in (and which is now a conveyer-belt towards the stocking of the various animal reserves as well as a launching pad for my trained animals) contains within its walls a very old cottage which several hundred years ago was inhabited by a succession of estate gamekeepers. In other words, the house has been built around the cottage.

The adjoining parklands and woods in which deer roamed virtually until our arrival, were breeding grounds and shooting acres for pheasants and other game. When the lions moved in, the pheasants moved out—to other parts of the vast Longleat domain, where they are still bred and shot, although it is noteworthy that some of them are returning to live in comparative peace among the African animals.

Gamekeepers are splendid professionals, whose knowledge in their field runs parallel to mine in some respects, and who therefore fascinate me. At Longleat they rear a large number of pheasants, feeding them and generally attending to their well-being from the time they are hatched out under a broody hen to the time the beaters are marshalled and sent out into the spinneys and woods to raise them in flight to be shot at sportingly. Their duties also include the protection of growing chicks from their feathered and four-footed foes, which are mainly magpies, jays, jackdaws, stoats, weasels and foxes. The fact that our lions sometimes stalked and killed a pheasant or partridge at Longleat was not a major problem. It only happened once in a while. Most of the lions ignored natural prey, being too lazy and well-fed to bother. And the young birds were raised well away from the reserve.

As always, there has been a certain amount of trouble with poachers at Longleat over the years and one had been particularly active about this time.

One lovely morning early in September I awoke very early and could not get back to sleep. There was a lot on my mind; I was fretting because we were getting low on hay and I had done nothing about it. One of the farms on the estate had a quantity on offer surplus to its requirements at a fairly reasonable price and I had a mind to go and look at it. Marquis was awake, too, one of his paws affectionately but heavily placed around my neck. Motioning him to silence, I slipped out of bed. Marquis followed, rising just like a cat, stretching with pleasure, gracefully releasing the last vestiges of sleep from his spine and shaking off the cares of the night from every part of his lithe young body.

I slipped on jodhpurs and sweater while he stood, motionless, waiting. We crept downstairs so as not to disturb Roger, David, nanny and cook, who would all expect to sleep for another couple of hours or so. The farm people would be up by the time I got there, as there was a mixed dairy herd to be milked.

Downstairs there were the delicious country smells of the kitchen in the rarified morning air—game fowl, shorn yesterday of their itchy feathers, hanging until the ultimate moment of ripeness . . . seven-pound jars of mincemeat already prepared to ferment towards winter festivals . . . pink ham fresh from the boiling, beautifully glazed.

There were cubs to attend to, while Marquis waited patiently, sitting as ordered in his rocking chair. And then we were off out into the crimson morning, lurching past the kennels and stables (whispering cautions of silence to the dogs and horses); out into the lane where swamps of leaves were already piling over the honeycombs of bank burrows amidst the rank, sharp odours of roots and nettles; across the edges of fields jagged with stubbles and scythe-hacked bean stalks; past piles of logs, sawn by forestry workers with such exactitude, that not one was a millimetre longer than the others; through woods where pigeons were beginning the day's love-mumurings and conkers were strewn on the withering turf.

Soon many acres of the fields, meadows, spinneys, copses

and great woods of the estate would be echoing to the sounds of beaters, armed with hazel sticks, yelling game to its destruction and it was also mushroom time, so I kept my eyes open for the tell-tale early morning signs as Marquis loped along by my side, off the lead because it was so early and we were unlikely to meet anyone until we got nearer to the cottages clustered round the farm.

Suddenly, there was a shot and then another. Marquis stiffened for a second, tail stuck out behind him like a pointer and then he was off like the wind into a thicket before I had any chance of restraining him by the collar. Almost at once there was an anguished cry and a man leapt from among the trees, a lurcher (which seemed a cross between collie, sheep-dog *and* greyhound) by his side, shotgun over his shoulder, and the two were off across the fields as if all the furies of hell were at their heels. But they need not have been quite so scared. Marquis was used to men and dogs. He was after something quite different. He had obviously seen a bird fall, although I had not, and in a moment he was back with a fat golden pheasant in his mouth. He made no objection when I took it from him.

Marquis had carried it softly and his teeth had not penetrated the bird's skin. He was partial to a bit of bird of any sort when we had some to spare, but obviously he was not going to be bothered plucking it and getting feathers up his nose or fleas in his ears. I decided to telephone the chief gamekeeper about the poacher on my return home but saw no reason why the plump hen pheasant should not be added to the birds in the kitchen larder.

Chapter Twenty-Three

MARQUIS AND THE GHOST

As he came up to his first birthday, our boy David was becoming the most photographed child in England, just as Marquis had been the most photographed lion cub. The *Daily Express* nominated The Pheasantry 'a sideshow better than the Stately Circus itself' after seeing 'rushes' from the now-completed BBC television series, and that brought the photographers around again in their hundreds. Inevitably, they all wanted 'Noah's Ark nursery' pictures and especially shots of David with wild cubs. This was easy. He was genuinely sharing his cot every day, for his afternoon nap, with twin lion cubs (a few weeks old) Twiggy and Sheba. There was no need for lullabies with this trio. They went off to dreamland together in a forest of intertwined arms and legs. David took them as much for granted as if they had been animated cuddly toys. He just did not know that it was unusual for a little boy to have such exotic playmates.

Twiggy and Sheba had been deserted at birth. They had lost a mother and gained a friend. And David had acquired two eager pupils. When David sucked his thumb, they sucked their paws. When it was bottle time it did not matter to any of them which bottle they consumed. In fact, David liked the vitamins the little lions got in their milk and their cod liver oil.

The trio's games were shared mainly by Shaun, the Great dane, Charles, the chimp, and J-J, the gorilla. Theirs was a secret world of play adults could not possibly understand or readily enter. If Marquis was around and they wanted a chase they would bop him on the nose to make him join in. At eighteen months, he was far too old for this sort of thing, or should have been. Indeed, the *News of the World* nominated me Britain's Bravest Girl for having such a mature man-eater around the house, and Father told them, 'I've warned her about that lion. He's now so heavy he'll break her bed one of these nights.'

Maybe Marquis was the largest lion anyone had ever kept at home, but to me he was still a child in affection or play. And often he acted like one. One day Roger donned a large lion-skin rug and crept downstairs to have a giggle in giving David and the pets a fright. Instead, he met Marquis in the hall and the great baby was nearly scared out of his handsome, still-spotted coat. First he hid behind his rocking chair and then he ran to me for reassurance and protection.

But I freely admit he *was* frightening in appearance.

As I have mentioned, Marquis adored travelling by car or in any vehicle. If he walked out into the yard and one of the family cars had its doors open, he would immediately jump in and growl to be taken somewhere. Early in November I took him up to London in Father's Rolls-Royce for a commercial engagement. As we were bowling along the M4 motorway towards London, he was lolling like royalty on a rug on the back seat and I was chatting away to him when a police Jaguar roared past me, its bell clanging, and signalled me to stop. Of course, Marquis at once sat up and took notice of the noise, so that when the two patrolmen came back to tell me I had been doing eighty miles an hour in a seventy limit, faced by a huge lion, they forgot their words of caution and could not get me on my way fast enough!

The occasion was the recording of an LP, by a pop group called The Trogs, in a London studio. They wanted the authentic roar of a king of beasts on a track entitled 'The Lion'. There was a strong table in the studio, so I made Marquis lie on it out of the way until his cue came up. The four boys in the group, Ronnie Bond, Chris Britton, Reg Presley and Peter Staples, were a bit nervous of him, as were the other 'hangers on', musicians, managers etc. in the studio, but all went well until the moment came for Marquis to give what passed for a roar, his voice not quite having broken yet.

A microphone was placed before Marquis, I gave him the signal, he raised his head and opened his mouth . . . But at that moment his nose touched the microphone which, for some reason, was 'live'. Not used to electric shocks, Marquis leapt in the air, the table fell over, the piano lid crashed down and, as I grabbed him by the collar, one of Marquis's front paws got caught in a chair, which he swung in all directions to get free.

Meanwhile, the name of the game in the studio was 'escape'. The Trogs, the musicians, the technicians and the others were heading for the swing doors like fieldmice in the path of a harvester. A photographer was flattened under the weight of an impresario. A dolly girl tried to claw her way through a locked door.

By the time they were all out in the street, Marquis was perfectly calm but nevertheless the artists' and repertoire manager decided to make use of the growl-like noise he had unwittingly taped when the microphone stung the lion, so we were able to escape back to Longleat earlier than anticipated.

Whether he had heard about this incident or not, I don't know, but when we arrived at another location a few days later to do a 'cat' commercial for Kosset Carpets, we found that the studio manager had driven stakes into the middle of the expensive carpets on the floor in order to tether Marquis securely wherever he happened to be needed!

It was quite a season for my regal friend. A film party had been laid on for 200 American and foreign show business writers at Longleat one day, but because of schedules running late, they were unable to take in the reserve, so Marquis was hastily pressed into service for the banquet at Longleat House. The film was *Far from the Madding Crowd*, with a world premiere to be attended by Princess Margaret, and among those present was its star, Julie Christie. Longleat was chosen partly because the film was shot in the west of England and partly because it was made by MGM, whose symbol is a lion.

The banquet was by candlelight, with Lord Bath as host, and was a very big success. It was the first occasion on which Marquis had spent any length of time in the ancestral home and I noticed that every time I led him past a certain passage (for like any cat he has to be taken out to the garden occasionally, especially after a bowl of champagne, which he lapped all too enthusiastically) he was unusually nervous and apprehensive, his hair bristling and his nose twitching. The passage was unusually cold, in a way that had nothing to do with the unusually warm October night outside—one of the maze of passageways that thread their way around the rambling hundred-room mansion.

Apart from the clammy cold air, there seemed nothing of note to distinguish it from the others, but it undoubtedly disturbed the lion emotionally and physically. Eventually, I dragged him past it for the last time, having been too busy to mention the experience to anyone. But a few days later, I happened to describe the incident to an estate worker who was having a cup of tea at The Pheasantry and who had been around the place for half a lifetime.

Before I had finished, he crossed himself rapidly, nearly knocking over his tea-cup.

'That would be the Walk, ma'am,' he said quietly. 'The Green Lady's Walk, they used to call it. They say it's haunted by the spirit of one of his Lordship's ancestors, Lady Louisa. They say as how her lover was murdered and she walks the corridor in grief.'

Although I know animals are extraordinarily sensitive to unseen and distant events, I am not a 'believer' in ghosts and such things. But the first chance I got I checked with the librarian and discovered that what I had been told was indeed one of many spooky legends surrounding Longleat. The Green Lady was Lord Bath's great-great-great-great-grandmother, who was Lady Louisa Carteret, daughter of the Earl of Granville, who married Thomas Thynne, the second Viscount Weymouth. The espousal turned out badly and she took a lover, whom she smuggled into Longleat, where the Viscount caught them in the act and, so the legend has it, killed the lover, whose body was said to have been buried in unconsecrated ground somewhere under the flagstones of the vast cellars of the house.

I also learned that, when the present Marquess was a young man and his father was having central heating installed, workmen came on the remains of a male under one of the cellars

—apparently a young man in Queen Anne style boots and clothing.

Whatever it was in that passageway, Marquis was aware of it and I was not. There is also a Thynne legend, apparently, that the family will be doomed to die out if the swans, which have nested by the stream for hundreds of years, should ever fly away and not return. I remember it now every time I see Longleat's swans circling The Pheasantry, as they quite often do. But I do not believe it.

Chapter Twenty-Four

OTHER AFRICAN ANIMALS

One morning I picked up a newspaper from the neat and comprehensive selection Roger always has laid out on a table in the sitting-room (neat until they are urgently needed in animal toilet-training operations, that is) and there on the front page was a cartoon about Longleat. It showed an English fox looking out of his lair at the lions and saying, 'Something's got to be done about immigration!' And I thought, dang me if he isn't telepathic!

We had been adding African creatures to our collection in the stockades we now had around the place, towards the time when the additional reserve would be ready, and that very morning a fox had got in and seized one of them—a crowned crane. The natives were striking back!

There are several good hunts around the area, and I ride with one of them when I get the chance (having first been 'blooded' at the age of twelve) but foxes are still a worry to us and it is constantly in my mind that one day one of them will carry away one of our exotic birds from the reserve. I am therefore always urging greater vigilance, but I fear that it will happen none the less. It is one of my few 'orphanage' worries.

At the end of November, 1967, permission was granted by

the Wiltshire County Council for us to more than double the size of the reserve by adding 115 acres of East African game park (to the north-east and adjoining the lion park, but separately fenced) with deer, zebras, giraffes and exotic birds. Heated quarters were to be built in which the animals would live at night. In the daytime they would be free, as would the public who were to be allowed out of their cars to picnic or stroll freely among the new animals. A monkey jungle was also planned for nearby. Inevitably there were objections, but the storm quickly died down. The plans included circulatory roads and a traffic management scheme for associated roads (to ease traffic congestion) plus a restaurant and toilets. These last were already proving a great money-spinner for Lord Bath, at about £1,000 a year in pennies. Maybe fear of the lions had something to do with the frequency with which the turnstiles clicked.

At the same time we were again thrown into frantic export-import activities by Father's decision to create three continental reserves—in Germany, France and Holland—all in country estates on fifty-fifty arrangements with titled owners, as at Longleat. And five more were pencilled in for the near future—Eire, Australia and Canada, plus Woburn and an estate in Scotland. We were not to be allowed to relax for a few years—that was certain.

Another very large consignment of animals for our projects arrived by sea at Avonmouth by the *Clan Menzies* from Mombasa—the most expensive ever shipped anywhere in the world. It consisted of twenty-five giraffes, thirty antelope, twenty crested cranes, eight elands, eight wildebeests, seven gazelle, six ostriches, five impalas, four dik-diks, three duiker and others—a real Noah's Ark of a ship, which had taken four weeks on the voyage. The total value of the animals was in excess of £50,000. The birds were transported direct to Longleat and the others were put in our Plymouth zoo, where complicated closed-circuit television equipment had been installed to give adequate twenty-four-hour-per-day surveillance during their fifty-six-day quarantine and also to allow visitors to see this unique collection of animals. Most of them had been trapped in the bush in Kenya or Uganda by Father and

Richard. Roger and I, too, had managed to do a bit of catching in the course of a holiday we had been able to snatch in the late summer. It was hoped that the giraffes, which were from one to two years old (against a life span of twenty years) would breed at Longleat. They are comparatively docile animals, unafraid of noise and not given to panic.

One of my favourite Chipperfield animal stories concerns a giraffe and my Uncle Dick (Father's illustrious brother, who still runs the family circus) and it happened in the depths of the Devonshire countryside one dark February afternoon.

We had a fine giraffe called George, who was exhibited for show rather than for training. A special house had been built for him and he had a keeper to himself, night and day in the early days until he allowed himself to be handled and paraded with a rider (sometimes me or one of my cousins or, when we could afford it, a beautiful coloured girl). George was unique in British circus acts and was a great favourite with all of us.

That February day, George was being driven along a country road in the dusk when suddenly one wheel of the waggon went into the ditch. Before anyone could reach it, the tall waggon had toppled on its side, and there it lay, with George in it, for five long hours. Nobody dared to get him out, in Dick Chipperfield's absence, in case he broke his neck or his legs.

It was raining and bitterly cold, I remember, and we had to take turns of comforting the poor animal, as best we could. By the time Uncle Dick arrived, we were in despair, fearing that poor African-born George would die of English-winter cold, if for no other reason. His keeper, a Nigerian, was so scared he forgot all his English and could only chatter to us in his native Yoruba.

But Uncle Dick was extremely resourceful and, almost as soon as he arrived, succeeded in persuading George to ease himself through the half-open door so that we could manhandle him onto the bank at the side of the ditch. So far so good. George lay shaking for half a minute and then, to our cheers, staggered to his feet and gave one of the men a hearty kick in the stomach to show that he was still very much alive. I don't even think the man minded, such was the relief we all felt.

We covered George in blankets, as it was still raining hard, and led him across the fields to a farm, the lights of which we could see, a mile or two away.

It must have been about eleven in the evening when we reached the farmhouse. Uncle Dick knocked hard at the door and eventually the farmer's head peered suspiciously out of an upper window.

'Do you mind if we put our giraffe in your barn for the night?' the irrepressible Dick Chipperfield shouted, without any preliminaries.

'Your *what*?' the farmer shouted back, disbelieving his ears.

'You heard!' said Uncle Dick.

There was then a lot of running about in the rambling old house, and we could hear broad Devonshire accents crying, 'What did 'e zay?' . . . 'Giraffe, m'dear' . . . and so on.

All ended happily. They could not have been more helpful, clucking away sympathetically when they saw George. Soon the tractor was moved out and George was installed in the barn. A stove was lit under him (he liked that) and everyone took turns of rubbing his ample frame, standing on step-ladders, to prevent him getting pneumonia. Meanwhile George, unconcerned again, ate well, and in the morning was as right as the rain which was still falling.

His waggon, righted in the morning light, was taken to him, and we drove off to rejoin the circus convoy, leaving a remote Devon farmer with a tall tale to tell his grandchildren, which it is doubtful if any of them would believe.

Work now went ahead quickly on the second reserve. The stream was dammed to form a water-hole (for the animals chosen for the new park drink a lot) and the giraffe houses were built alongside. Digging began too on the foundations for the three miles of road which would wind around this park.

Of necessity, we advertised at this time for more 'white hunters'. 'What's this?' asked the newspapers. 'Have the original ones been eaten?' And a Punch contributor went one better, and said, 'I'm glad I'm not a regular at the Bath Arms when the safari truck rolls up to disgorge a pack of grizzled men in khaki shorts, who spend the evening swilling sundowners and bellowing hunting yarns at each other—"caught one of the natives trying to smuggle anchovy sandwiches out to the cubs. I made short work of *him*, I can tell you." I wonder if the Race Relations Board could not be persuaded to look into the Marquess's activities.'

In fact, 'white hunter' is a widely used job title in the animal business. There's no reason why white hunters should not be black as long as they are experienced.

While we were overworked and understaffed, we were nearly caught out by a Candid Camera television crew. One day an amazing 'caravan' of jeep-type vehicles rolled up to the gates, each bearing a party of safari-clad hunters with guns. I happened to see them pass The Pheasantry as I was grooming my horses. So I hopped on a pony's bare back and rode the short distance to the reserve entrance just in time to stop the gatemen opening up to these impressive-looking creatures 'We've come to shoot some lions,' the leading hunter was shouting for the benefit of a hidden microphone. 'Then you must be that rotten Candid Camera lot,' I shouted back, and that was the end of one safari. They trundled back to London with no film footage worth showing.

Organization at The Pheasantry was becoming more complex every day, but efficiency is Roger's middle name, so nothing went very wrong despite an almost crippling workload. One of my so-called tools, to keep tabs on the many animals (at Southampton and Plymouth as well as at Longleat) with which I was now concerned, was a 'Pregnancy Board' in the kitchen—a blackboard on which details of pregnancies, births, illnesses and animal events generally could be chalked. As the different categories of mothers in my care have varying gestation periods, it could never be a simple chart. Chimps are nearest to humans, with an eight-month pregnancy; lions take sixteen weeks; elephants twenty months . . . and so on.

An added hazard, connected with the 'Pregnancy Board', which can produce riotously funny or frighteningly serious responses in apparently normal conversations, is that many of the animals are named after members of the family or of the firm.

A statement on the telephone to the effect that 'Miss Mary has had a miscarriage', can cause consternation.

Or maybe Father will drop by and I'll say, casually, 'By the way, Dad, Isobel's pregnant.'

'Hell!' will be my father's rejoinder, as he contemplates the idea of an office without a secretary.

'Not Isobel Baird,' I tell him. 'Isobel Giraffe!'

'Great!' he'll say then.

If it had been the former, it *would* have been hell. As it's the latter, it's great.

These mixed-up conversations can have their aspects of fear.

One day towards the end of 1967 I met my father at the door of The Pheasantry, tears in my eyes, and told him, 'Marjorie has just died.'

Father went white. 'How could she?' he cried. 'I was with her a few hours ago.'

He thought it was his sister. It was a lioness.

The chimpanzees on Man-Ape Island had begun to breed by this time, a fact with which we were particularly pleased. We kept adding to the colony as suitable animals became available, the latest recruit being a four-year-old, Max, who had spent his entire life in the circus and who now became island 'schoolmaster', daily teaching remembered tricks to the others. This saved us the trouble (in fact it is a well-known method of training chimps) and gave added pleasure to the visitors on the lake. Max is a great extrovert and, when not swinging about on ropes, trapeze and in trees, can be depended on to give a welcome to the public—chattering, waving his arms, grinning and hopping up and down to earn the applause he has grown to expect from his circus days.

We had had Max in The Pheasantry for a bit before he had been taken out to the island and he had been very reluctant to leave. More than Charles or any other chimp we had had in the 'orphanage', he had struck up an astonishing friendship with Marquis—so much so that the large lion was forever bounding about with 'jockey' Max on his back. Alas, the chimp was getting to the age when it might not be safe to have him free around the house. There was always the danger that sex would rear its ugly head and make him vicious. So poor Max had to be drugged (he would not have gone otherwise) and taken to the island where he was gradually introduced to his playmates.

Late one still, cold winter night some four weeks after Max's banishment, I was sitting more or less alone in The Pheasantry, Marquis by my side, writing up my diary, when a fiendish scratching and wailing began at the back door. I was petrified. Roger was away in Plymouth and would not be back until very late. But when I looked at Marquis, I knew it could not be anything too terrible. He was alert but calm and cheerful. It was obviously someone he knew and he indicated to me that we should go to the door.

I took Marquis by the collar and, not knowing what to expect, eased the heavy door open a few inches on the chain and peered out.

At once all was made clear. There, in the pitch darkness, was a pair of pink-rimmed, milky-white eyes and the largest set of grinning teeth imaginable. I burst out laughing, the sight was so unexpected and irresistible, and slipped the chain. It was unmistakably Max. He bounded in, gave me such an affectionate hug and went off to play with Marquis, who was just as pleased as Max at the renewal of their friendship.

A few minutes later, a sheepish-looking keeper arrived and explained that Max had been brought to the mainland (to which move he did not object) on a chain fastened to the keeper's wrist, to have a wound dressed. But he had slipped the chain as soon as he was ashore and had loped off to The Pheasantry faster than anyone could follow.

I allowed Max to stay with Marquis overnight, but it was heartbreaking, the next day, to have to tranquillize the cheerful chimp once more and ship him again to his new home. Alas, with animals you often have to be cruel to be kind.

Chimps are incredible escape artists. They can pick locks or escape from any strait-jacket devised. Only their fear of water allows us to keep our breeding colony safe on the island.

Chapter Twenty-Five

MARQUIS ACHIEVES LIONHOOD

Just before his second birthday, Marquis began to roar properly for the first time. He had been trying for months, but it would not quite come. Then suddenly he got it right and from then on we were treated to ever-more-ferocious roars almost every time we looked his way. He had got past his adolescence and he was showing off like mad.

In other ways, too, it was obvious that Marquis was all-male and well into his 'teens'.

There are neurotic young lions a-plenty, whose sexuality is all in the head, who live fantasies (as if they were *Playboy* patrons) and *do* nothing. Marquis was not one of them. His masculinity was coming to a head in a marvellous calm maturity and he made it simply plain to me that he wanted a lioness. He loved me, yes. But I was his mother-companion. He needed something more. He was young but he was ready. And in such moments, when he looked long into my eyes, I knew he expected me to choose for him a mate, or preferably mates (for lions are naturally polygamous) as healthy, beautiful, sensual and sexy as he was.

Marquis was not yet ready to go out into the reserve. Father was still worried about me because, in his long experience, he had never come across a 250 pound domesticated lion before. But I had no fears about Marquis. Most unusually among the many cubs I had raised he exhibited no desire whatever to leave home. I was thankful about this, because I was not ready for his move either. He just wanted to be the gay bachelor, living at The Pheasantry, enjoying his 'green' years for a bit longer with a bit of casual love-making between spells of sleep, play and home cooking.

His new need showed up in spells of restlessness and prolonged watchfulness. On hearing the roar of a lioness in the park he would rise to his magnificent full height and roar back for all he was worth, looking reproachfully at me the while for having failed to understand or implement the messages he had been throwing to me. Or he would sniff around (from pillar to post, as it were) seeking the odour of a female in season. Or he would strain at his chain, hearing sounds that were outside the range of my ears.

I understood only too well what was the matter with him, and I was giving it as much thought as if I had been a marriage-arranger in some eastern country. But it was not easy to resolve. The four main prides in the park were settling down well and should not be disturbed. The lionesses of his age we had raised in The Pheasantry were unsuitable, or had moved on, or were due to move on soon.

I was not in any way jealous of his sudden virility, but it thrilled me to know that he was ready to breed so early and I was determined that his wives should be worthy of him.

So I made a number of secret match-making trips to Plymouth and Southampton, looking around the new stock being prepared for transfer to Longleat. And, among the lionesses due to leave quarantine, I found several particularly attractive young specimens. I then made my decision.

I would set up a harem for Marquis *near home*.

This was no sooner thought of than done. I called in some skilled labour and had the largest of our Pheasantry outbuildings reinforced, made lion-proof, and rendered comfortable with straw. I then put Marquis's rocking chair in a corner and encouraged him to sleep in it there after meals instead of in the dining-room. All the while I talked to him about my plan, relating the outbuilding in sign language to the roars of lionesses in the nearby reserve.

'This is going to be your very own mortgage-free home,' I more or less signalled. 'And your brides will be here any day.'

After a few days of this, I went to Southhampton in a safari waggon and brought back three splendid young lionesses I had chosen from the 'possibles'. Their names were Lady, Vicerene, and Countess, and in this respect, as in their looks and temperament, they were suitably grand to be espoused to my lion. Equally importantly, they had all got on well together when sharing a cage in quarantine.

While Marquis was chained up in the office with Roger, I let the three girls loose in the new den, having temporarily removed his rocking chair again. They immediately got the smell of their husband-to-be from the straw and whined their interest. The building was about a hundred yards from the house, screened by other buildings and walls, but Marquis, before he could actually hear the lionesses, obviously sensed their presence (Roger told me afterwards) and was the very devil to restrain.

It was now necessary to give the girls a few days to settle in before letting Marquis loose on them. But it was also important that nothing should be hidden from him . . . that he should know that the days of his fulfilment were at hand.

So when I took him for his walk later on in the day of their arrival, I led the astonished and delighted Marquis within eye-shot and ear-shot of the harem, confirming in reassuring words that the three girls were exclusively for him, while letting them have their first view of their own very majestic lord and master.

Marquis behaved splendidly, immediately sensing and neutralizing my fear that he might break away towards them and disgrace me in front of some of the workers. In fact, he stood tall in grace and power, pulling gently but firmly against the chain and sizing up, from a dignified distance, the lionesses, as they paced in front of the mesh of the door. On this occasion, not one of the four raised a murmur. In silence, Marquis allowed himself to be led on up the path towards his duck pond and the swim he still enjoyed more than anything. In silence they watched him go, knowing that very soon he would return.

It was a beautiful spring afternoon and my heart was singing. I was not losing a son, as the saying goes, I was gaining three daughters.

We can learn so much from the animals. Marquis splashed

around in a completely relaxed way, as if it were a perfectly normal morning. He showed no impatience. He had taken in the situation immediately; he was leaving the details of the marriage ceremony and the honeymoon to me.

The elegance and ease of movement of a creature that is free from mental or physical tension is beautiful beyond description. Watching Marquis settle down beside me for a snooze, and then rise out of sleep in a magnificently relaxed show of grace was bliss. The danger in having raised him for so long as a member of the family had been that he might have adopted some of my characteristics. That there was no sign of neurotic pro-human behaviour at this turning-point in our lives together was, I felt, a compliment to me as well as to him. I take a fairly simple, *animal* view of life. If I had passed this on to Marquis, rather than the tensions that screw up so much of the human and animal world, then I was proud and delighted. Thus was I achieving fulfilment through him, as I had achieved it in my own life, and in a way he was reaching it through me.

I also took the three lionesses separately for walks. They were not tame, in the way that Marquis was tame, but they behaved well, showed intelligence, sensibility and sensitivity, giving me still more hope that they would produce cubs worthy of Marquis's unique nature and personality.

Within a few days, it was apparent to me that Lady was in season. She showed it in the usual ways. And on his next walk up the lane, Marquis confirmed it for me. We had not gone far until he pulled like mad on the chain, following some female pugmarks, and began excitedly sniffing around a bush as if it was festooned with goats' meat, crooning, snuffling, chuckling and grunting the while. It was the bush where Lady had placed her jets, with their message that Marquis instantly understood.

I could delay the nuptials no longer, as the average lioness is on heat for only four days at a time. I called out Roger and Richard, to stand by in case of a jealous fight among the females, and then set Marquis loose in the outhouse—in his new home among his new wives. There was no more commotion than might have been expected at such an introduction. All four had been fed earlier. The females were on the drowsy side. Marquis went immediately to Lady and they were circling each other excitedly as I closed the door.

I stood chatting to the men nearby for a time in case trouble developed, but all was quiet, except for coo-ings and purrings, apparently from Marquis and Lady.

All that afternoon and night I could concentrate on nothing. My mind was alert in case things went wrong in the harem. But, apart from several ecstatic muted roars from Marquis, the honeymoon seemed calm and normal—more so than mine had been!

In the morning, as I went into the stable to see to the horses, Marquis called to me. It was his usual calm cheerful greeting, pitched just loudly enough for me to hear. I dropped everything and went to him. He was so pleased to see me and obviously wanted to boast of his new experiences. I opened the door and let him out. The lionesses were all asleep. But before I shut them in again, and took Marquis out into the quiet of the park where he could tell me all about his first night of marriage, I glanced at Lady, whose 'seasonal' smell was strong on the morning air. She had blood on her marmalade-coloured body and legs from claw marks; and she had the signs of bites on her head and shoulders. Without question, she had been mated more than once and probably sired successfully. Biting and scratching are a normal and apparently enjoyable part of the climax of the sex act with lions, an act which can be repeated as often as eight times in twenty-four hours. By his purring (and the relaxed depth of her sleep), it was apparent that Marquis had been a major success as a lover. I patted his huge head and grinned my pleasure at his pleasure as we trotted off to gambol and gossip among the buttercups and dandelions of a typically English scene.

His coupling had been an experience but not a turning point. It had raised no barriers between us. He obviously did not care that he would now be living a double life. Royal beasts are above such things. What was it the Bible said about the flesh profiting nothing and only the spirit conquering? Marquis obviously subscribed to that . . . so maybe he was a Christian lion!

Thus ran my thoughts as we now bounded towards Marquis's pond, a splash-bath obviously foremost in his mind.

There were no hang-ups or let-downs. The trust and confidence between us were crackling away merrily as before. My fulfilled and kingly lion had no intention of leaving 'home' yet awhile. His wives would have to realize that their lord and master had a well-established and loved queen mum.

There were many things we still had to learn together and we could now get on with them again. We reached the crooked tree by the pond. Marquis looked up at me and licked my hand with his huge rough tongue. 'You're a rascal,' I told him as I playfully cuffed his ear, and slipped his chain. 'You're a rascal, but you're loved.'

Happy endings are too final. This was another happy beginning in an uncomplicated continuing relationship.

Famous Animal Books in Fontana

Joy Adamson
The Spotted Sphinx *(Illus.)*
Born Free *(Illus.)*
Living Free *(Illus.)*
Forever Free *(Illus.)*

George Adamson
Bwana Game *(Illus.)*

Gerald Durrell
Birds, Beasts and Relatives
Two in the Bush
Rosy is My Relative

Jacquie Durrell
Beasts in My Bed *(Illus.)*

Virginia McKenna
Some of My Friends Have Tails *(Illus.)*

E. P. Gee
The Wild Life of India *(Illus.)*

Bernard and Michael Grzimek
Serengeti Shall Not Die *(Illus.)*

Susanne Hart
The Tame and the Wild *(Illus.)*

Buster Lloyd-Jones
The Animals Came in One by One

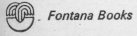 *Fontana Books*